life's

about

relationships

DR. DON WOODARD

life's

about

relationships

A Foundation

for Good Relationships

AMBASSADOR INTERNATIONAL
GREENVILLE, SOUTH CAROLINA & BELFAST, NORTHERN IRELAND

www.ambassador-international.com

Life's About Relationships

A Foundation for Good Relationships
©2021 by Dr. Don Woodard
All rights reserved

ISBN: 978-1-64960-046-2
eISBN: 978-1-64960-047-9

Cover Design by Hannah Linder Designs
Interior Design by Dentelle Design
Digital Edition by Anna Riebe Raats
Edited by Megan Gerig

Scriptures taken from the King James version of the Bible. Public Domain.

All definitions are from Webster's 1828 dictionary.

AMBASSADOR INTERNATIONAL
Emerald House
411 University Ridge, Suite B14
Greenville, SC 29601
United States
www.ambassador-international.com

AMBASSADOR BOOKS
The Mount
2 Woodstock Link
Belfast, BT6 8DD
Northern Ireland, United Kingdom
www.ambassadormedia.co.uk

The colophon is a trademark of Ambassador, a Christian publishing company.

Dedicated to my brother Edward D. Woodard.

You know me well and love me anyway.

Contents

Foreword

When Dr. Don Woodard first told me about the new book he was writing, I was excited. From the very first moment of our existence, we find ourselves struggling to figure out this new world outside the womb as a doctor lays us on our exhausted mother. As we begin to grow, we lean on people like parents, teachers, friends, and pastors to help us make sense of the world around us. Life truly is all about relationships!

I was honored that Dr. Don would ask me to write a foreword to such a helpful book. I met Dr. Don Woodard many years ago at a church leadership conference in Southington, Connecticut. I was barely out of Bible college and was the youth pastor for a rural church. The church had no teens at the time but had a vision for growth. Why they brought me in, I'll never know. I had no plans to be a youth pastor. I wasn't the stereotypical wild and zany guy who connects well with young people in a cool and hip way. But there I was.

As I wandered around a gym that hosted table after table of exhibitors at the conference, I found Dr. Don Woodard behind a table filled with materials dealing with youth ministry. We struck up a conversation, and I walked away with several helpful resources that would prove to be a blessing in my ministry.

I decided I would attend his breakout sessions at the conference. In a way, I kind of felt obligated; however, as I listened to these sessions, I received more than just practical lessons and great advice. I received a look into his heart. You could tell this was a man who cared about the people in that room—including me. That was powerful.

In the following years, I have gotten to know Don quite a bit more. I count him as a mentor and a co-laborer in the gospel, but also as a genuine friend. If there was anyone qualified to write a book on relationships, I assure you, this is the guy to do it. There are few people in the world that love people more than him.

I'll start this foreword by confessing, I love Facebook. I spend way too much time posting, checking out memes, and yes, getting into debates. I've even gotten into other social media platforms such as Twitter and Instagram. As I interacted with people over social media, however, I began to see the false senses of relationship, intimacy, and life purpose that the online platforms gave.

According to Facebook, I have hundreds of friends. According to Twitter, I have hundreds of followers. But what does that even mean? Life online gives me the ability to project an image of myself that I want others to see. I show them the "me" that I wish I was. But the truth can be far from it.

For example, I could post a beautiful picture of my family—everyone smiling and looking thrilled. But, what you did not see the minutes before and after the picture were my kids punching each other, my angry words at everyone, and my wife about to give up in exhaustion. You see what I want you to see, and the same is true of you. When I see you online, I see only what you want me to see. I don't see the real you, and you don't see the real me. We are simply pictures without depth and ultimate meaning.

Often our online relationships create a false sense of intimacy and knowledge. I know one temptation I fall prey to often is that of the internet crusader. I pick a cause, political or theological, and start posting like crazy! In my own mind, I'm contending for the faith, but in reality I have to ask myself, "Is my trolling really impacting people?" It's easy to mouth off behind a keyboard without seeing a facial reaction, looking someone in the eye, or even hearing an immediate reaction.

My point in all of this is to stress the need for cultivating actual relationships with actual people. Relationships that are mutually beneficial and loving. In other words, *real* relationships! The principles found in the book will help you do that. The social media age has made a book like this a needed addition to your bookshelf.

I am grateful that Dr. Don wrote this book, as it will be a help to many people. As he weaves his way through the Biblical account of the very first relationship between Adam and Eve and God, you will find his advice practical, easy to understand, and honoring to God. I hope you will go through the following pages slowly and thoughtfully. Take time to stop and pray when you feel convicted about a certain area and use Dr. Don's advice to work on the many relationships in your life. After all, life is about relationships!

KEVIN THOMPSON

Kevin Thompson is the host of the Basic Bible Podcast and currently serves as the Bible teacher at Rock County Christian School in Beloit, Wisconsin. In the past, Kevin has served as an Assistant Pastor, Youth Pastor and Elder in several local churches in the Northeast and Midwest. He holds a Master of Theology degree from Liberty University and an undergraduate degree from Pensacola Christian College. He is married to his wife Jill. Together they have adopted four boys and thus have their hands and quiver full.

CHAPTER 1

Life Is About Relationships

Have you ever considered that some of the most important blessings in your life are attached to a relationship? Not a place, not an object, not material wealth, but a relationship with another human being. And have you ever considered that most of your challenges in life are attached to a relationship?

Life is about relationships!

Webster's 1828 dictionary defines relationships as the state of being related by kindred, affinity, or other alliance. Our kindred would be those we are related to by birth, adoption, or marriage. Personally, I also include my Christian family in this category because we are connected through Jesus Christ. Related by affinity would include those we are united with through interests, employment, housing, shopping, and education. If we wanted to take affinity to the extreme, we could say that we are related by affinity to all people since we all live on the same planet. An alliance would be a connection or union through a common cause or purpose such as being on the same baseball team or a member of the same fraternity or college.

Occasionally, disagreements, harsh words, or too much time apart challenges our closest relationships. During these times, our best relationships need adjustments. By practicing Biblical relationship principles, we can make the needed adjustments to find reconciliation and enjoyment in our best relationships and improve our not so great relationships.

God Created You for a Relationship

We will investigate this in more detail in a separate chapter, but I want to touch on it here. Before God the Trinity (Elohim) created the first man, Adam, the Trinity met to discuss the creation of man. Genesis 1:26 tells us, *"And God said, Let us make man in Our image, after Our likeness..."* The creation of man was the most important act in all of creation because the first man was created to have a relationship with God. Just as the Trinity conversed before they created the first man, I believe that they converse before the conception of every human being created. The conversations amongst the members of the Trinity serve to exemplify the importance of communication in our relationships, and they remind us that God created us for a relationship with Him.

The Trinity Is a Relationship

In Genesis 1:1 we read, *"In the beginning God created the heaven and the earth."* The word for God here is Elohim, which is the plural use of the word God denoting the Trinity. The Trinity consists of three persons: God the Father, God the Son, which is Jesus Christ, and God the Holy Spirit. We know from Scripture that all three were present at the time of creation and each one had a part in creation: God the Father planned the creation of the world, the Son performed the work of creation (*"all things were made by Him"* - John 1:3), and the Spirit of God empowered the creation (*"the Spirit of God moved"* - Genesis 1:2). In their relationship today, the Trinity sustains their creation. In Jesus' prayer to the Father recorded in John 17:5, He says, *"And now, O Father, glorify Thou me with Thine Own Self with the glory which I had with Thee before the world was."* This helps us understand that Jesus Christ had a loving relationship with God the Father and the Holy Spirit, *"before the world was,"* and further confirms that the Trinity is a relationship.

God's Basic Laws and Precepts of Life Are About Relationships

The first four Ten Commandments are about our relationship with God. I have abbreviated them here:

- Thou shalt have no other gods before me.
- Thou shalt not make unto thee any graven image.
- Thou shalt not take the name of the Lord thy God in vain.
- Remember the Sabbath day and keep it holy.

The remaining six commandments are about our relationships with others:

- Honour thy father and thy mother.
- Thou shalt not kill.
- Thou shalt not commit adultery.
- Thou shalt not steal.
- Thou shalt not bear false witness.
- Thou shall not covet.

Matthew 22:37–40 reads, *"Jesus said unto him, Thou shalt love the LORD thy God with all thy heart, and with all thy soul, and with all thy mind. This is the first and great commandment. And the second is like unto it, Thou shalt love thy neighbor as thyself. On these two commandments hang all the law and the prophets."*

In these two commandments, Jesus summarizes all the Ten Commandments given in the Old Testament. Notice the statement, *"hang all the law and the prophets."* The word "hang" means to rest on, to be supported by, to continue in. Jesus is teaching here that the most important things in life are supported by and continue in these two commandments.

Our Relationships Matter Most

At the end of our lives, we will not say I wish I would have spent more time at the office or playing sports or seeking fortune and fame. We will wish that we would have spent more time with family, with those that we love. Money, possessions, and health can all fade away or lose their value, but two things are certain: our relationship with God, Who loves us and created us for Himself, and those special lifelong relationships that God sent into our lives to make our life more pleasant and interesting. When everything else is gone, these relationships will matter the most.

Life Changing Relationship Principles Can Change Your Life

I would have been a much better husband and father when Debbie and I began our family if I would have known and practiced what you will read in these pages. Although we all sometimes fail, I make a sincere effort to practice these principles in my relationships now, and they have helped me be a better man, husband, father, grandfather, leader, and minister of the Gospel. My prayer is that they will help you make your strongest relationships even stronger and make the struggling ones better. It is never too late to learn, and it is never too late to improve yourself or your relationships. Life and relationships are a continual learning experience!

CHAPTER 2
We Need Each Other

I once read a story about two porcupines in Northern Canada. They were cold so they decided to huddle together to get warm. When they huddled together, they were warm, but their quills jabbed each other, so they moved apart. Before long they grew cold again, so they huddled close and were soon jabbing each other again. Same story, same ending, they needed each other, but they kept needling each other. So it is in our lives. We need each other's companionship, but we often needle each other.

The First Human Needed a Human

Genesis 2:18 says, *"And the LORD God said, It is not good that the man should be alone; I will make him an help meet for him."*

Companionship was the primary reason God created the Woman for the man. (There is a reason I refer to Eve as the "Woman" that I will reveal later). God saw that man needed someone similar yet different from him, so He created the Woman and the two became one in marriage. This was the first relationship between two human beings. Although it has been debated for centuries, I believe the evidence is clear that God created the man to need a woman and the woman to need a man. The following is a list of needs I've compiled over the years that every married couple should seek to fulfill in their marriage relationship:

A wife's relationship needs from her husband:

- Unconditional love and security

- Emotional communication
- Spiritual intimacy
- Encouragement and affirmation
- Companionship and understanding

A husband's relationship needs from his wife:

- Respect and unconditional love
- Sexual intimacy
- Companionship and understanding
- Encouragement and affirmation
- Spiritual intimacy

As some men and women were created without a desire for sexual relationships, I believe that not everyone was created for, but that all people still need, the companionship of friends.

We Need Mentors for Personal Growth

Long before I realized what a mentor was, I had mentors in my life. In my mid-twenties as I was just beginning my ministry, Dr. George Prinzing had a very positive influence on my life. I sought his counsel on marriage, family, finances, and ministry. I never realized how much I depended on him until he passed away at the young age of sixty. Even today, however, I often talk about the lessons I learned from Dr. Prinzing, and I find myself passing those lessons on to the younger men that I now mentor.

None of us are self-made, and we don't grow emotionally and spiritually without positive nurturing from good relationships. My friend Charlie "Tremendous" Jones said, "You will be the same person in five years as you are today except for the people you meet and the books you read." We need mentors to help us grow in our relationships, our vocations, our finances, and our walk with God. Mentoring others also can not only help us grow even more but give us the opportunity to invest in the lives of others. Proverbs 1:5 says, "A wise man will hear, and will increase learning; and a man of understanding shall attain unto wise counsels."

The following are Biblical examples of mentoring:

- Titus 2:3–5 - *"The aged women likewise, that they be in behaviour as becometh holiness, not false accusers, not given to much wine, teachers of good things; that they may teach the young women to be sober, to love their husbands, to love their children, to be discreet, chaste, keepers at home, good, obedient to their own husbands, that the word of God be not blasphemed."*

- 2 Timothy 2:2 - *"And the things that thou hast heard of me among many witnesses, the same commit thou to faithful men, who shall be able to teach others also."*

- Psalms 71:18 - *"Now also when I am old and greyheaded, O God, forsake me not; until I have shewed Thy strength unto this generation, and Thy power to every one that is to come."*

We Need Each Other for Strength

Success in life requires moral, emotional, and spiritual strength. No matter how confident we are, we still need companionship to provide us with the strength to keep pressing on. Sometimes we are the one in need of strength and sometimes we are the ones instilling strength. As Proverbs 27:17 says, *"Iron sharpeneth iron; so a man sharpeneth the countenance of his friend."*

Ministers are often the ones giving emotional and spiritual strength to others, but there are times when the minister needs strength. Such was the case for me when our grandson died. My family and friends were looking to me for answers, for strength, and for comfort. Conducting my own grandson's funeral was the most difficult thing I've ever done. Thankfully, during this time of grief, my friend Danny Arnold came to my side. He prayed with me, talked with me, and stood by me. Danny was a source of emotional and spiritual strength for me while I was trying to give strength to those who needed me.

We Need Each Other to Achieve Our Personal Goals and Desires.

In his book *The One Minute Manager*, Ken Blanchard said, "None of us is as smart as all of us." To achieve the things we desire in life, we need the encouragement, love, affirmation, and companionship of others. We not only need these things from others, however, but we also need to offer them to others. Looking back on my own life, I have had many "encouragers" along the way. Helen French, whom I call my second mom, has been cheering me on for nearly fifty years now. Because of her ability to help me think through an idea, she has helped me pursue several goals and has also kept me from even more mistakes. She has also taught me the importance of encouraging other people to achieve their goals and desires.

As Ecclesiastes 4:9–12 says, *"Two are better than one; because they have a good reward for their labour. For if they fall, the one will lift up his fellow: but woe to him that is alone when he falleth; for he hath not another to help him up. Again, if two lie together, then they have heat: but how can one be warm alone? And if one prevail against him, two shall withstand him; and a threefold cord is not quickly broken."*

We Need Each Other for Spiritual Growth and Stability

As a follower of Christ, I am convinced that the most important relationship in our lives is our relationship with God through Jesus Christ. To continually grow in this relationship, I not only need my daily, personal, private worship time with God, but I also need the companionship and edification of like-minded believers. I need relationships with others that I can bond with on a spiritual level and serve with in a common cause.

The best source of this companionship is in a Christ-centered church. A good church will help you find spiritual mentors that can teach you more about God's Word and how to deepen your relationship with Christ. Dr. Floyd Radebaugh and Pastor Ron Douglas have been a tremendous source of stability in my life. My dear friend Dr. Tom Wallace has been a mentor to me for over twenty years now, he is nearly ninety years old now, but is still going strong for God. I have called Dr. Wallace many times and I have driven to his home in Tennessee to meet with him and seek his counsel. And my friend Dr. Charles Keen, has influenced my life spiritually for nearly forty years now. He taught me the importance of searching the Scriptures to guide my decision-making in my personal life, in my relationships, and in my ministry. He also taught me the importance of encouraging my co-laborers in the ministry and in life. All of these men have uplifted me in times of crisis and have taught me to have a deep love for the Bible. Each day I try to pass on the spiritual lessons I have learned from them.

> Hebrews 10:24–25 - *"And let us consider one another to provoke unto love and to good works: Not forsaking the assembling of ourselves together, as the manner of some is; but exhorting one another: and so much the more, as ye see the day approaching."*

We Need Each Other to Overcome Our Past Sins and Mistakes

We all fail, make mistakes, stumble, and sometimes even fall. When this happens, we need encouragement and love and sometimes even rebuke from a friend or loved one. Too often in Christianity, people who fall or make big mistakes are cast aside and or are limited in what they can do to overcome their past regrets. It will do us well to remember that God used the Apostle Paul in spite of the regrets of his past. Paul wrote to Timothy, *"And I thank Christ Jesus our Lord, Who hath enabled me, for that He counted me faithful, putting me into the ministry; Who was before a blasphemer, and a persecutor, and injurious: but I obtained mercy, because I did it ignorantly in unbelief. And the grace of our Lord was exceeding abundant with faith and love which is in Christ Jesus. This is a faithful saying, and worthy of all acceptation, that Christ Jesus came into the world to save sinners; of whom I am chief. Howbeit for this cause I obtained mercy, that in me first Jesus Christ might shew forth all longsuffering, for a pattern to them which should hereafter believe on Him to life everlasting"* (1 Timothy 1:12-16).

I've had the pleasure of disciplining scores of people who had fallen spiritually and got back up. When someone falls our desire should not be to run to their side and kick them while they are down, but we should desire to reach down, offer to help them up, and give them a shoulder to lean on to press forward. This is what we would want if we were the one who had fallen, and this is what we should do for others.

Proverbs 10:12 - *"Hatred stirreth up strifes: but love covereth all sins."*

1 Peter 4:8 - *"And above all things have fervent charity among yourselves: for charity shall cover the multitude of sins."*

Galatians 6:1–2 - *"Brethren, if a man be overtaken in a fault, ye which are spiritual, restore such an one in the spirit of meekness; considering thyself, lest thou also be tempted. Bear ye one another's burdens, and so fulfil the law of Christ."*

We Need to Forgive and We Need to Be Forgiven

Because we do fail and we do offend one other, we need to know that forgiveness is possible and available to us. We need affirmation that there are people in our lives who will love us unconditionally and offer us that second and third chance. We also need to be prepared to forgive in such a manner.

Years ago, I remember talking with an elderly man whom I will call Jim. He would not accept Christ's gift of eternal life and salvation because he said he could never forgive his older brother. As I listened to Jim tell the story of his relationship with his brother, his father, and the land inheritance, Jim told me that he had done something in his youth that angered his father, something that his father never forgave him for. Jim's brother then used the incident to convince his father to give him all the land instead of dividing it between the two sons. Without realizing it, Jim's bitterness toward his father for not forgiving him caused him to treat his brother the same way. The good news is that after several conversations with a good pastor, Jim was able to accept that assurance of his deceased father's forgiveness could not be obtained, but God's forgiveness could be. Jim accepted God's forgiveness, forgave his brother, and became a Christian.

> Ephesians 4:31–32 - *"Let all bitterness, and wrath, and anger, and clamour, and evil speaking, be put away from you, with all malice: And be ye kind one to another, tenderhearted, forgiving one another, even as God for Christ's sake hath forgiven you."*

Don't Unite with Unbelievers

One of our biggest mistakes in relationships is choosing friends and associates that don't hold the same values, core beliefs, and attitudes that we hold. Although we can't choose our relatives, we can choose the level of influence they have in our lives, and we can choose how we treat our family even when there are challenges. We can also choose our friendships, and when we choose our friends and associates, we need to choose those who will be a positive influence and who will hold to the same core values and attitudes we possess.

I once tried to help a young lady whom I will call Melody. This young lady had grown up in a very dysfunctional family. She lacked personal confidence, and her self-value was extremely love, but she was very intelligent and beautiful. Unfortunately, Melody was dating a young man named Tim who dragged Melody down even more. Because of her relationship with Tim, she was in a constant state of confusion, guilt, and despair.

I explained to her that if she wanted to grow in her walk with Jesus Christ and commit to positive change in her life, she needed to walk away from her relationship with him. After realizing that Tim was not committed to her, she walked away from her relationship with Tim. Relationships with unbelievers only hinder the spiritual and emotional progress of a believer. Once Melody realized this and instead focused on growing her relationship with Jesus, she was stronger, happier, and more content than ever.

2 Corinthians 6:14 - *"Be ye not unequally yoked together with unbelievers: for what fellowship hath righteousness with unrighteousness? and what communion hath light with darkness?"*

We Are Known for the Way We Treat Each Other

Whether it is in our family, social, or business relationships, we are known for the way we treat others. For example, when we speak of others, we say, "Bill is a good man. He is always friendly." Or "Jim is hard to get along with." Or "Teresa has such a sweet personality." Or "Tina is a great mom."

For a short time in my early twenties, I worked for a man I will call William. All of us employees knew that whenever William called a team meeting, he was going to yell about how no one was working hard enough. Even when our team was performing well and business was good, William was never satisfied. He never congratulated anyone on a job well done, he never encouraged an employee for making a good effort, and he never spoke kindly to anyone. He was known for treating people badly, and eventually, it caused him to lose his position at the company.

Our reputations are built on our treatment and interaction with each other. When interacting with another person, we should follow the golden relationship rule, "Do unto others as you would have them do unto you."

Matthew 7:12 - *"Therefore all things whatsoever ye would that men should do to you, do ye even so to them: for this is the law and the prophets."*

John 13:35 - *"By this shall all men know that ye are my disciples, if ye have love one to another."*

Like the two porcupines, we sometimes jab each other, but we still need each other. Begin improving your relationship with others by improving yourself and trimming your own quills.

CHAPTER 3
First Relationships

Most of our first memories, whether good or bad, are connected to a relationship. Many of us are blessed to have good first relationship memories. Some of my first memories are of my mother and me in a small upstairs apartment by a set of railroad tracks in Marion, Ohio. One vivid memory is us sharing a meal at the kitchen table. We were making funny faces at each other and laughing until our bellies hurt. It is a good memory, and one that I won't forget!

In theology, there is an interpretive principle of studying the Scriptures referred to as "The Law of First Mention." The basic idea of this principle is that the first mention of anything in Scripture is significant because it gives that topic a foundation.

When it comes to relationships in Scripture, the first mention of a relationship is God's relationship with Himself. We see this relationship in the first two chapters of Genesis, especially when God refers to the Trinity during the creation of man in Genesis 1:26: *"And God said, Let us make man in our image, after our likeness: and let them have dominion over the fish of the sea, and over the fowl of the air, and over the cattle, and over all the earth, and over every creeping thing that creepeth upon the earth."*

Our relationship with ourself is important, and it is from our first relationships that we learn about ourselves. It is where we learn to relate to others and where we develop core personal beliefs about our value, self-confidence, and perspectives of life. From our first relationships, we also learn about trust, giving us the foundation on which we build future relationships.

The next first relationship in Scripture is God's relationship with the first man, Adam. Adam and Eve had a good beginning in their relationship with God. God loved them, He sought to bond with them in the Garden of Eden, and He trusted them, giving them dominion of the garden, *"And the Lord God took the man, and put him into the garden of Eden to dress it and to keep it"* (Genesis 2:15). Even when they trespassed against Him, God reconciled with them. We can take from this that Adam and Eve's first relationship with God was a good experience.

Unfortunately, not everyone's first relationships in life are good. For over thirty-five years I've counseled young people who have struggled to overcome the lasting effects of their early relationships.

My wife and I began counseling a woman whom I will call Linda. Linda's mother was a drug addict who sold her body for drugs. When Linda was eleven years old, she and her three younger siblings were placed in foster care. Sadly, Linda's foster care experiences were not all positive. Now, Linda is in her sixties, and she still struggles with relationships. She has very few friends and does not trust anyone. She has a low self-value, and no self-confidence. She hates God and views herself as broken and rejected by God and society.

People who don't know Linda's history probably ask themselves, "What's wrong with her?" She can be abrasive, offensive, and distant from people, but Linda is not a bad person. She truly wants to find happiness, but she is afraid of it and does not believe she can ever obtain it. Why? Because Linda's first relationships were negative, she developed a self-defense against being hurt in relationships! She was wounded at a young age by her first relationships, and medication can't heal that. Linda has told Debbie and me that we are the only people she trusts. Sadly, she rejects the truth of God's redeeming love that could transform her life. We continue to express God's unconditional love to her and pray that she will be saved and allow God to heal her hurts.

Can You Recall Your First Relationship Memory?

Is it pleasant? Is it a confirmation of love, joy, and security? If it is, then you are blessed. Take a moment and be thankful!

Is your first relationship memory unpleasant? Is it possible that you have challenges in your current relationships that are connected to your first relationship memories and or experiences? Please consider the following suggestions.

We Can't Change First Relationships

We don't choose our family. Linda could not change her first relationship, and she could not change the circumstances that came with those first relationships. However, she does have the power to change her perspective of those relationships, as difficult as that can be.

I urge you to live in the present! None of us can change how our lives began, but we can live today to the fullest and we can make the most of our current relationships and our future relationships. Although many people have experienced very painful past relationships, choosing to change your perspective and forgive those who hurt you can help you to have more self-value, self-confidence, and better relationships now. Forgiveness will be discussed in detail later but consider the importance of it now. Consider forgiving those that may have created your first bad memories.

A Lesson for Parents

Our early relationship with our children is crucial. Be there for them, bond with them, invest time in them, express interest in them and the things that they are interested in. Nurture them, build their self-confidence, affirm their value to you, and forgive of their trespasses. Teaching them the importance of their relationship with God and pouring your love into them will give them the guidance they need to develop good relationships all throughout their life!

A Lesson for All of Us

Although, there are no perfect families, some of us were blessed with wonderful first relationships. We had parents who loved each other and us, parents who were emotionally stable and secure in themselves, their vocations, and their personal relationships. We can learn from them because they helped us become who we are today. For those of us who were not blessed with loving parents, we are blessed in knowing that we can still value the good relationships we have today.

Linda's parents are gone, and like all of us, she cannot change the way her first relationships began. But, we can change our perspective of them, and we can improve our relationships today!

Our First Relationship Memories Don't Have to Define Who We Are Today

Because of the hurt she has experienced in her first relationship, Linda has grown bitter and distrustful toward relationships. Sadly, she has not realized that despite her bad first relationship memories, she can have good relationships today. If you have wounds from your first relationships, you don't have to allow them to define who you are today or the relationships you have today! Determine in your heart who you are, know that God created you for a relationship with Him, and remember that He has a purpose for you. God has given you the power to determine who you are. Let that define you and not the memories of bad first relationships.

Your Next Relationship

Your next relationship could be an opportunity to help someone heal from relationship wounds. Your next relationship could be an opportunity for you to influence someone to live their dream. Your next relationship could be an opportunity to mentor someone or to find a new mentor for yourself. Even if you have experienced bad relationships in the past, do not let those define your relationships now. Choose today to pour yourself into your next relationship. It could be life changing, if not for you, then for the other person.

CHAPTER 4

Your Relationship with Self

"What a gloomy thing, not to know the address of one's soul."

Victor Hugo

"Examine yourselves, whether ye be in the faith; prove your own selves . . . "

2 Corinthians 13:5

Have you ever noticed that most people that don't get along with others usually don't like themselves either? In studying the Scriptures, I have concluded that our two most important relationships in life are with God and with ourselves. If those two relationships have issues, then all our other relationships will have issues.

The biggest giant to confront in life is our self! King David is an example of this. We know from Scripture that as a shepherd boy David confronted a lion and a bear and killed them both. We also know he is famous for slaying the giant Goliath with a slingshot and the power of God. All of these were amazing victories that required a great amount of courage, but perhaps the biggest giant David ever confronted was when he asked God to look into his own heart to know himself. In Psalm 139:23 David prayed, *"Search me, O God, and know my heart: try me, and know my thoughts."* David knew that God would give Him understanding of himself and would reveal to him what he needed to improve in himself. In order to improve our relationship with our self, we must know about ourselves. To do this, I offer some questions to ask yourself. Questions that God asked various people in the Bible. Questions that required these people to know themselves.

Where Are You?

After Adam and Eve realized that they had disobeyed God, they hid and covered themselves with aprons made from fig leaves. God came to them and asked, "Where are you?" God knew where they were, but God was making Adam be accountable for himself.

In the same manner, we must be accountable for ourselves. Where are you in your personal accountability? Where are you in your spiritual and emotional life? Where are you in your relationship with God and with yourself? We must ask ourselves these questions and answer them honestly if we are to know about our relationship with ourselves. It is in the answer to these questions that you will find direction. If you are not where you should be in your journey of life, make it your goal to get there. Enlist the help of family, friends, your pastor or spiritual mentor. Search the Scriptures and seek God's leading.

Who Told You That?

Let's look at this question in two parts. Adam's answer to God's question, "Where art thou?" was "we were naked so we hid ourselves." Then God asked, "Who told thee that thou wast naked?" (Genesis 3:9–11).

Well, who told Adam and Eve that they were naked? Their conscience! We have within ourselves, a "self-awareness," our inner man, that we call a conscience. So, ask yourself, "What does your conscience tell you?"

The second part is to ask yourself, "Who told me the things I believe about myself and about my life?" A friend of mine named Joe had a father who was an alcoholic and was physically and emotionally abusive. He repeatedly told Joe he was nothing. He cursed him almost daily, told him he would never accomplish anything, that he was a foolish dreamer, and that no one would ever want him or love him. Thankfully Joe's mother sent him to a good church, where he was surrounded with people that believed in him and encouraged him to do his best. Eventually, he came to realize that the lies his father had told him were not true. Joe took the time to search his own heart and the Scriptures and pray about the lies he had come to believe. Because of God's love for him, Joe came to forgive and love his deceased father. Today, he focuses on the good memories of him, and seldom says anything bad, or negative about his father.

So, ask yourself, "Who told me the things I believe about myself? Are they true? If they are true, what do I need to do to make positive changes to myself? What do I believe about myself that is not true? What do I need to do to overcome believing the things that are not true?"

Consider for a moment that you may not have a good relationship with yourself because you believe lies about yourself that other people have told you. Did people who really know your heart tell you the things you believe about yourself? Did people who are happy with their own lives tell you those lies? Most likely those people don't really know you and are miserable with themselves. If you are struggling with this, I recommend that you talk with a Biblical counselor. I would also suggest memorizing the following verses:

> Psalms 139:14 - *"I will praise thee; for I am fearfully and wonderfully made: marvellous are Thy works; and that my soul knoweth right well."*

> Philippians 1:6 - *"Being confident of this very thing, that He which hath begun a good work in you will perform it until the day of Jesus Christ."*

> Philippians 4:13 - *"I can do all things through Christ which strengtheneth me."*

> 2 Timothy 1:7 - *"For God hath not given us the spirit of fear; but of power, and of love, and of a sound mind."*

On the other hand, if you know in your heart that you need to work on your anger, self-confidence, or some other area, ask your spouse, pastor, or other spiritual mentor to help you.

What Are You Angry About?

When Cain's offering was rejected by God, God asked Cain, "Why art thou wroth?" (Genesis 4:6). Wroth means very angry, provoked, and embittered. Anger is a major cause of struggles in our relationships. If we harbor anger toward people from our past, that anger will affect our current relationships. If we harbor anger toward ourselves over regrets, failures, and mistakes, that anger will negatively affect our relationship with ourselves and with others. The Bible says in Proverbs 14:10, *"The heart knoweth his own bitterness . . . "* I offer the following list of issues we commonly harbor anger over. The list is not exhaustive, but it will help us see how anger can affect our relationship with ourselves and others.

- **Hurt**: Proverbs 18:14 - *"The spirit of a man will sustain his infirmity; but a wounded spirit who can bear?"*
- **Betrayal**: Psalms 41:9 - *"Yea, mine own familiar friend, in whom I trusted, which did eat of my bread, hath lifted up his heel against me."*
- **Frustration**: 2 Corinthians 4:8 - *"We are troubled on every side, yet not distressed; we are perplexed, but not in despair."*
- **Failure**: Proverbs 24:16a - *"For a just man falleth seven times, and riseth up again . . . "*
- **Disappointment**: Proverbs 13:12 - *"Hope deferred maketh the heart sick: but when the desire cometh, it is a tree of life."*
- Unreasonable expectations: Psalm 42:11 - *"Why art thou cast down, O my soul? and why art thou disquieted within me? hope thou in God: for I shall yet praise Him, Who is the health of my countenance, and my God."*

If you are struggling with anger issues, look into your heart, find the root of the anger, and remove it from your heart. Removing the anger is easier said than done, but the following Biblical process can be helpful. Ephesians 4:31 says, *"Let all bitterness, and wrath, and anger, and clamour, and evil speaking, be put away from you, with all malice."* And Colossians 3:8 says, *"But now ye also put off all these; anger, wrath, malice, blasphemy, filthy communication out of your mouth."* The process for removing anger from our heart is found in the statements, "put off" and "put away from you." I often tell people who struggle with anger that although they may not have been the one who planted the seed of anger in their heart, with God's help, they have to be the one to pull it out by the root. To "put off" or "put away from you" is to remove the anger from your heart and thrust it away from you. To put it out of your heart and let it die. Without a place to grow and without us nurturing the anger it will die.

Removing the anger may also require forgiving those who planted the seed of anger, which we will address in Chapter 16: Trespasses.

Where Are You Going?

God is not as concerned about where we came from as He is about where we are going Although where we came from does matter, we should be more focused on the present and the future than we are the past. We cannot change our past, but we can be intentional about our life in the present and we can set goals and chart a course of action for our future.

In Genesis 16:8, God asked Hagar, "Where will you go?" Hagar knew where she came from, she knew who and what she was running from, but she had no plan as to where she was going. As I enter my sixties, I look back and am in awe of where God has allowed me to go, of the people He has placed in my life, and of the things He has allowed me to be involved in. And yet even at sixty, I must ask myself, "Where do I go from here?"

Ask yourself, "What are my goals and what desires? What path am I on and where will it lead me?" An important part of your relationship with yourself includes where you came from, but more importantly, where you are right now and where you are going!

What's in Your Hands?

One of my favorite leaders in the Bible is Moses. Not only was he a great leader, but he also was a great servant of God. In Genesis 3, God appears to Moses in the burning bush and tells him to confront Pharaoh and lead the Israelites out of bondage from the land of Egypt. Moses's response to this were all the reasons why he was not qualified for the task. "I'm not anyone that Pharaoh or the Israelites would pay attention to. They won't listen to me or believe me. I'm not a good speaker I have a speech impediment." To these objections, God responds with a question that required Moses to know himself. "What is that in thine hand?" The point is that while Moses was focused on his inabilities and weaknesses, God was focused on Moses's abilities and strengths.

In your relationship with yourself, it is important that you know your abilities and your strengths. Know what is in your hands and know how to use what you have to serve God and others!

Who Is on Your Team?

Another objection Moses gave to God was, "Please send someone else." To this God responded, "Is Aaron the Levite your brother? I'm sending you Moses, but I will send Aaron with you, he will be your spokesmen and his heart is for you" (See Exodus 3:14–16).

A Levite was someone who had a zeal and commitment to God. Moses then had someone on his team who was committed to God and also had a heart for Moses. As you think about your relationship with yourself, your goals, and your future, ask yourself, "Who is on my team? Who loves God and loves me and will lift me up?"

Are You Carrying Unnecessary Baggage?

The Apostle Paul instructed, *"Let us lay aside every weight, and the sin which doth so easily beset* (enclose) *us, and let us run with patience the race that is set before us"* (Hebrews 12:1b).

Notice that Paul separates weight from sin. A weight we are carrying may not be a sin, but it can hinder our progress. Another word for weight could be baggage. This baggage could be bad experiences from past relationships, wounds, acts of betrayal, abuse and bad relationship behaviors learned from others. You may be thinking of something right now that has happened in your life that weighs you down.

Baggage in your life will hinder your relationship with yourself and with others, and the heavier the baggage, the more it will hinder you. So, ask yourself, "What is hindering my progress?" When you learn what the baggage is, lay it aside and press on! My process of "laying aside the weight" is finding a quiet, private place to pray. I tell God about the baggage I know I am carrying and that I need to lay aside. I then mentally, emotionally, and spiritually leave the baggage at that place. I have even pretended like the weight was on my shoulders and taken both hands and cast the "imaginary" baggage from off my shoulders into a field or into a lake. After doing this, I try not to return to that place.

The Answers to the Questions

I once heard a minister suggest that we ask ourselves these last three questions to help us determine our purpose and desire for life.

- What do you think about? When you are alone with your thoughts, what is the primary thing you dwell on, what is the one thing you desire to accomplish with your life?
- What do you sing about? What makes you happy, what brings joy to your heart that causes you to sing?
- What do you cry about? What grieves you about your own life or the lives of others? What injustice do you see in the world that you would like to influence for change? What would you like to improve in yourself or your relationships?

These are excellent questions that will help you in your relationship with yourself! It is important to keep in mind that it is not the question that will help you to know yourself, but it will be the answers to those questions that will help you know what's in your heart and your thoughts. It is only when we know what's in our hearts that we can truly know ourselves.

CHAPTER 5

Create Your Own World

The Genesis account of creation begins, *"In the beginning God created the heaven and the earth"* (Genesis 1:1). The chapter continues with God creating the sun, moon, stars, the firmament, land, grass, trees, vegetation, and all animal life. This is not a detailed description of what Genesis 1:1–25 tells us, but the truth for us to focus on is that before God created man, He created a secure, fruitful world with everything that would be needed for a lasting and meaningful relationship.

God's purpose in creating man was for a relationship. Ephesians 2:10 says, *"For we are His workmanship, created in Christ Jesus unto good works, which God hath before ordained that we should walk in them."* God's purpose in creating the world was for man to have a place to develop that relationship. Consider the wisdom in this, God did not create man then try to create a world for the man to live in. He created the world first.

Here is the principle of this relationship lesson: create your world first then seek to build a life relationship. By world, I'm referring to your personal life, your existence, your personality, your character, and your attributes. You might think, but I have been married a while or I've been in a relationship for a while. What can I do? My answer to that is simple: create a better world. No matter where we are in our relationships, we can always improve ourselves, and we can always improve the world we are creating. D. L. Moody is credited with saying, "The biggest room in the world is the room for improvement."

Let's dive into some principles for creating your world or improving your world.

Have a Good Relationship with God

Our relationship with God is the foundation on which we build all other relationships in life. As we commented earlier, God created us for the purpose of a relationship, and He has already initiated a relationship with us by creating a world for us and by giving His only begotten Son, Jesus Christ, to be our redeemer. The way we complete the relationship is by realizing we need God and by believing on Jesus Christ as our Saviour. John 1:12 says, *"But as many as received Him, to them gave He power to become the sons of God, even to them that believe on His name:"* It is turning to Jesus Christ in faith that brings us into a relationship with God. Once you have that relationship, continually build and strengthen your relationship with God and all other relationships in your life will begin to improve.

Know Who You Are and Know What You Can Offer

Most of us seek what we can *get* out of a relationship instead of what we can *give* to a relationship. God does not ask a lot from us, but He does offer a lot to us. He offers unconditional love, communication, forgiveness, abundant life, stability, and much more that we cannot humanly comprehend. Looking at our own relationships, we must know our strengths and our weaknesses to know what we can offer in a relationship and what we must guard against distracting our relationships. The other important aspect of knowing who you are and what you can offer is that you can use this knowledge to grow and make a sincere effort to improve yourself. By doing so, your relationships will improve.

Have a Firm Set of Principles to Follow

When you select your life principles, consider how those principles will affect others in your life. Will your life principles enhance your relationships? Some people are deceived into thinking that something is wrong with everyone else because no one can seem to get along with them, when in fact the problem is not everyone else, the problem is them! The reason for this is they do not have a firm set of life principles to live by. If your life is not guided by firm principles, your lack of principles will manifest in your closest relationships. Seek the Bible for the best source of life principles to follow, and those principles will enhance your relationships.

Have a Clear Vision of the Kind of World You Want to Build

On October 1, 1971, five years after Walt Disney passed away, Disney World had its grand opening. During the dedication ceremony, someone turned to Mrs. Walt Disney and said, "Isn't it a shame that Walt didn't live to see this?" Mrs. Disney replied, "He did see it, that's why it's here" (Mike Vance, Creative Director at Disney). This story contains a great truth about having a vision for our lives. I certainly don't pretend that I know the mind of God, but I'm confident that God envisioned the kind of world He wanted to create for the first man before He ever created the heaven and the earth.

In like manner, we must envision the kind of world we want to create for our relationships. The young adult who is searching for his or her life mate should envision the type of world they want to create for that person. Although Mr. Disney created a fairytale kind of world, the principle holds true: we should have a clear vision and a desire to create a world that will make our relationships all that they can be. What vision do you have for your closet relationships?

Create a Secure You

Most of us desire leaders that are stable and secure in who they are and where they are going. A stable person will create a stable world, and an unstable person will create an unstable world. All of us need secure, stable relationships, and if we ourselves are secure, we can help create better relationships.

Be secure in who you are emotionally by strengthening yourself spiritually. Anger, jealousy, bitterness, strife, and similar emotions will cause unstableness and will affect our relationships. If you are struggling in a close relationship, ask yourself: Am I or the other person dealing with any unstable emotional issues? If you suspect there are issues, address them.

The World God Created Has Seasons

One of the blessings of the world God created for us is the four seasons. Each new season brings change and each season has its own beauty. My personal favorite season is spring. I love the newness of life, the grass beginning to green, the trees coming to life with leaves, the flowers blossoming, and the weather warming. As God's creation has seasons so will the world we create for our relationships.

We notice this most in our marriage relationship and in our relationship with children. My wife Debbie and I have gone through the season of our youth, we have gone through the season of rearing our children, and now we are in the season of enjoying grandchildren. In the coming years, we will enter the season of old age. Sometimes we are faced with difficult seasons. When the difficulties come, just be patient, remain focused on the person you love and weather the season you are in.

Perhaps one of the most difficult seasons our family has weathered together was the death of our grandson Caleb who died in the womb just weeks before his due date. Only through prayer, love, and affirmations of God's peace and comfort were we able to get through the difficult season. God was gracious to us, however, and our daughter gave birth to a beautiful little girl about a year and a half later. As you endure hard seasons, remember that spring is coming!

Take Dominion of Your World

When God created man and put him in the world He had created for him, He instructed the man to "Be fruitful, and multiply, and replenish the earth, and subdue it: and have dominion . . . " (Genesis 1:28). There are two important words here, the first is "subdue," which means to conquer, and the second word is "dominion," which means to control. These are some of the first instructions God gave to man, and these instructions contain some very important truths about life and about relationships. In order for us to conquer the world we are creating, we must first conquer ourselves. And in order for us to have dominion over the world we are creating, we must have control over ourselves.

A lack of control over one's self is a sure way to cause relationship challenges. When we don't have control over our personal emotions, behavior, temperament, actions and reactions then our world will be out of control and issues will develop in our relationships. The best example of this is when the Woman lost control of herself and ate of the forbidden tree. Genesis 3:6 states, *"And when the woman saw that the tree was good for food, and that it was pleasant to the eyes, and a tree to be desired to make one wise, she took of the fruit thereof, and did eat, and gave also unto her husband with her; and he did eat."*

We see here that the Woman ate the forbidden fruit because it was pleasant to the eyes and was a tree to be desired. She rejected what God had told her and relinquished dominion of herself and her world to the serpent that had intruded her world. The consequences of this were severe. In Genesis 3:16 God told the Woman, *"I will greatly multiply thy sorrow and thy conception; in sorrow thou shalt bring forth children; and thy desire shall be to thy husband, and he shall rule over thee."* Genesis 3:23 says, *"Therefore the Lord God sent him forth from the garden of Eden, to till the ground from whence he was taken."* Adam and the Woman lost control over the world they had in the Garden of Eden because they lost control of themselves. Dominion of your world begins with dominion over yourself.

Maintain the World You Create

When God placed man in the Garden of Eden, He told Adam to "Dress it and to keep it" (Genesis 2:15). The word "dress" has the idea of work or till the ground, to serve. To maintain good relationships in our world, we must serve those we love, and we must continually cultivate our own spiritual lives. The word "keep" has the meaning of to hedge, guard, or protect. This is very important; we must protect the world we create. In the Garden of Eden, God had created a perfect place for man then gave them dominion and freewill to make choices. They chose to allow the Serpent to enter into a conversation with them. Through deceit and persuasion, he caused havoc and division in the relationships between the Woman, Adam and God. Always protect the world you are creating.

Create a World That Will Replenish Itself

When God placed man in the Garden of Eden, He said, *"Let the earth bring forth grass, the herb **yielding seed**, and the fruit tree **yielding fruit** after his kind, whose seed is in itself, upon the earth: and it was so. And the earth brought forth grass, and herb yielding seed after his kind, and the tree **yielding fruit, whose seed was in itself, after his kind**: and God saw that it was good"* (Genesis 1:11–12). Notice the underlined words. Every living thing that grows from the earth has some kind of seed or spore whereby it reproduces itself, after its kind.

God created the world to replenish itself after its kind. The world we create should be one that replenishes itself with love, grace, mercy, understanding, justice, hope, service, humility, patience, truth and life. For a world to reproduce these attributes, these attributes must be sown with them. We must sow these attributes by our own behaviors, by the way we treat those closest to us, and by those we invite into our world and share our world with.

What Are Characteristics of the World That You Are Creating?

If we realize that the world we have created is not the best it can be, we can make adjustments, beginning with our own attitudes and behaviors. If you are not content with the life you are living or the world you are creating, it's not too late to make changes or improvements. Begin with improving yourself, work on your relationship with God and with yourself, and you will find that your other relationships will follow and your world will improve.

CHAPTER 6

Trust

Breaking trust is like breaking a fine piece of China into many pieces—it is very difficult to glue back together again. Without question, trust is the most important component in any relationship. Once trust has been broken, it is challenging to restore. Trust is defined as confidence, reliance or resting of the mind in the integrity, veracity, justice, friendship, or other sound principle of another person.

Trust and faith are synonyms as trust can also be defined as faith on a personal level. For example, I have faith that I could take my car on a three-thousand-mile journey, but the reason I have faith in my car is because I trust my mechanic who does the maintenance and repairs on my car. Trust is faith on a personal level! If we trust a person, we always have faith in what that person tells us.

Genesis 3:1 might be one of the most solemn verses in the book of Genesis, *"Now the serpent was more subtil than any beast of the field which the LORD God had made. And he said unto the woman, Yea, hath God said, Ye shall not eat of every tree of the garden?"* What Satan was doing in the Garden goes much deeper than Satan attacking what God had told Adam and the Woman. Satan was attacking God's trustworthiness!

The serpent persuaded the Woman to doubt God. Satan knew that if he could convince the Woman to distrust what God had told her and Adam, then they would turn against Him. This was an attack on the relationship God had created Adam and the Woman for. There is nothing more important than honesty and trust in a relationship. Deceit, lying, and deviousness will always break trust. A friend must be able to trust a friend, a wife must be able to trust her husband, a husband must be able to trust his wife, a child must be able to trust his or her parent, a parent must be able to trust his or her child, and a follower must be able to trust his or her leader.

God Earned Man's Trust

Just as trust is the most important component in a relationship, maintaining that trust is equally important. From the beginning, God was proactive in earning Adam and the Woman's trust. We can learn from God's example. The following points are some principles on how we can earn trust in our relationships.

We Earn Trust by Focusing on the Person

From the beginning, all that God did for Adam and Eve was for them and their needs. Because He created people for a relationship, God's relationship with mankind is the most important thing to Him. For us to establish trust in our relationships, we must persuade the people in our lives to believe that they are important to us, and we must work at maintaining the world we created for them. Someone wisely said, "People remember the way you make them feel, when people feel that they are important to us, when they sincerely believe we are focused of them and their well-being they will be more trusting of us." God met the needs of Adam and the Woman by planting a garden for them and placing everything they needed in the garden. We earn trust by meeting the needs of the other person to the best of our ability.

We Earn Trust through Companionship

God daily came to Adam and the Woman to walk with them in the garden. I personally believe that God was available to them anytime Adam and the Woman desired His presence, just as He makes Himself available to us today through prayer and the Bible. To earn trust in our relationships, we must make time for companionship. We must show the person that they are important to us by taking time to listen, by sharing their interests, and by investing time with them.

We Earn Trust by Honoring Boundaries

God told Adam and the Woman of the offenses that could strain the relationship between Him and them. Having clear boundaries is an important value in our most intimate relationships. We must express the things that would be trespasses against us, and we must honor the other person when they express trespasses against them. Expressing and honoring one another's boundaries builds trust.

We Earn Trust by Listening

When Adam and the Woman disobeyed God by eating of the forbidden tree, they went into hiding, yet because they were both important to God, He came to the Garden and called out to them, "Where art thou?"(Genesis 3:9) Being God, He knew where they were, but He wanted to give them an opportunity to speak for themselves. Notice in Genesis 3 that after God asked where they were, He was silent. God was letting them speak while He listened. We earn trust by listening.

We Earn Trust by Keeping Our Word

God told Adam and the Woman that if they ate of the forbidden tree they would die. After they ate of the forbidden tree, He took them out of the Garden and they eventually died. He kept His word. We must understand the value of trust and the consequences for breaking trust. We earn trust by keeping our word even when it is difficult.

We Earn Trust by Being Honest

Did your parents ever tell you, "Always tell the truth. You will be in more trouble if you lie"? Be honest even when it hurts. The serpent began his relationship with Adam and the Woman by being dishonest. He is the great deceiver and his dishonesty caused a major problem in Adam and the Woman's life.

Dishonesty always causes problems in relationships. We see the benefits of honesty in the way God approached Adam and the Woman after they had eaten of the forbidden tree and confronted them about their disobedience. He did so in an honest and forthright manner, and in turn, Adam and the Woman were honest with God. The honesty brought about a resolution and reconciliation. Honesty is the best policy in our relationships, and we must always begin by being honest with ourselves and with God.

We Earn Trust by Making Sacrifices

The fact that God desired reconciliation after Adam and the Woman went against what He had specifically told them not to do amazes me. Not only did God come to where they were, but He is also the one that made a sacrifice to reconcile the broken relationship. Genesis 3:21 tells us, *"Unto Adam also and to his wife did the LORD God make coats of skins, and clothed them."* God sacrificed an animal, probably a lamb and probably one lamb for Adam and one for Eve. The lives of these animals were sacrificed to cover their nakedness. The point I want to emphasize here is that God made the sacrifice for them, He did not ask them to sacrifice anything. There are numerous applications here, but the one we look to now is that in order to build trust in any relationship and especially in our closest relationships, we must be willing to make sacrifices. We must be willing to forgive trespasses, we must be willing to put away our anger, we must be willing to serve the other party when they are not able to carry their load, and we must be willing to love like God loves, sacrificially and unconditionally.

We Earn Trust by Giving Trust

When God placed Adam and the Woman in the Garden of Eden, He expressed trust in them by telling them that everything they needed was in the garden and by giving them the assignment to dress it (cultivate) and to keep (maintain and protect) it (Genesis 2:15). God expressed that He trusted Adam and the Woman with the garden that He had created for them. We can earn trust by showing trust.

We Earn Trust by Giving People the Opportunity to Be Productive

God told Adam and the Woman to "be fruitful and multiply" (Genesis 1:28). We know He was telling them to have children, but He was also giving them the opportunity to be productive themselves. God could have created children for them, but He gave them the opportunity to produce on their own. It is interesting that we earn trust by not only being productive in our own lives, but also by giving people the opportunity and the tools necessary to be productive and successful themselves.

We Earn Trust by Letting People Make Their Own Decisions

In Genesis 2;19 God entrusted Adam with the responsibility of naming all the animals. When people such as children are in our care, we often must make decisions for them, but we also have a responsibility to teach them to make right decisions. By giving them the opportunity to make good decisions, we can show our trust in them and can build their trust in us.

Take the time to examine your own relationships, especially the closest ones. Are you building trust? Have you broken trust? Trust can be restored! Begin by picking up the broken pieces and start gluing them back together.

CHAPTER 7

The Purpose of You

"And God said, Let us make man in our image, after our likeness . . . " (Genesis 1:26a). God the Father, God the Son, and God the Holy Spirit had a conversation before They created the first man. The human being They were going to create was the reason for everything else They had created up to this point.

I have heard well-meaning people say that God created man solely for the purpose of worshipping Him in fear and trembling, living in constant fear of God's wrath so that man would serve Him. They would go on to make the argument that God is a heartless, unloving Being that wants to punish man all the time if we don't measure up to His demands. There is no evidence of this in Scripture. God does desire our worship, but it is because worship is a vital part of our relationship with Him.

We see in Genesis 1:26 that God did not decide on a whim to create man. It was His plan all along, His purpose of creating the world. He wanted to have a relationship and commune together with man. When God the Father, God the Son and God the Holy Spirit decided that They would create a man in Their own image, after Their own likeness, They were referring to man being a soul, spirit, and body.

Why was it important for God to create man like Himself? Because God desires to have a connection with you, to form an alliance with you, and to develop a relationship with you. God has made every provision for this to be possible because this is the purpose for which He created you.

God Created More Humans for the Purpose of Relationships

When God saw that it was not good for the man to be alone, He decided to make a helpmeet for him. Adam looked upon the woman God had created for him and said, *"This is now bone of my bones, and flesh of my flesh: she shall be called Woman, because she was taken out of Man"* (Genesis 2:23). The word "woman" means part of me. In most marriage lectures, the emphasis is usually placed on the word "helpmeet." Although that is a relevant point, I don't remember anyone ever teaching on the importance of the meaning of the word woman.

The woman was like the man, yet she was created for the purpose of a relationship with the man, to be a companion to him. She was part of him, yet she was her own person. Consider your closest relationships. My wife is part of me, my children are part of me, and my son-in-laws and daughter-in-laws are part of me. My grandchildren are part of me. My brother and sisters are part of me. The people in my church family are part of me. I believe this is one of the reasons we grieve when we lose a close loved one, they have become part of us, part of who we are. God created us to be part of each other's lives.

God Formed You for a Relationship

God literally spoke the world into existence, but when it came time to create man, the Bible tells us, *"And the LORD God formed man of the dust of the ground, and breathed into his nostrils the breath of life; and man became a living soul"* (Genesis 2:7). God formed man, which means God made, molded, planned, and constituted man. You did not evolve, you are not here because of a big bang or because two atoms collided in the atmosphere billions of years ago. God formed the first man in His own image after His likeness for the purpose of a relationship.

> Isaiah 44:2 - *"Thus saith the LORD that made thee, and formed thee from the womb, which will help thee; Fear not . . . "*

Isaiah 44:24 - *"Thus saith the LORD, Thy redeemer, and He that formed thee from the womb, I am the LORD that maketh all things; that stretcheth forth the heavens alone; that spreadeth abroad the earth by myself."*

Jeremiah 1:5a - *"Before I formed thee in the belly I knew thee . . . "*

Jeremiah 29:11 - *"For I know the thoughts that I think toward you, saith the LORD, thoughts of peace, and not of evil, to give you an expected end."*

My friend, God created you and you are part of Him. More than anything, God desires that you have the relationship with Him that He created you for. You are God's purpose!

CHAPTER 8

The Breathing Life Principle

We all know someone that can just take the life out of the room or drain the life out of you. Draining the life out of people should not be our purpose, but rather, we should breathe life into others. Genesis 2:7 says, *"And the LORD God formed man of the dust of the ground, and breathed into his nostrils the breath of life; and man became a living soul."*

Imagine a lifeless body that all of a sudden comes to life. This is the way John Gill describes what took place in Genesis 2:7. Mr. Gill writes, "And breathed into his nostrils the breath of life; which in that way entered into his body, and quickened it, which before was a lifeless lump of clay . . . " (*Exposition of the Old Testament*). No words were spoken in Genesis 2:7. God was breathing spiritual life into man. This is what separates man from the rest of creation—man is a living soul and man is a spirit and has a body. We don't have the power to breathe life into other human beings and make them a living soul and give them a spirit; however, we do have the power to breathe life into their spirit, and unfortunately, we have the power to drain the life out of their spirit.

We Can Breathe Healing into a Wounded Spirit

Scripture speaks of having a "broken heart" (Psalm 147:3) and a "wounded spirit" (Proverbs 18:14). Both of these are the results of challenges and trials in life and are often the result of negative relationship experiences. When we know this is the case, we can try to breathe healing into the spirit of the wounded and broken hearted.

We Breathe Life through Prayer

One of the best things we can do for those who are dear to our heart is to call their name out to our Heavenly Father every day. Make it part of your daily schedule to pray for your loved ones, asking God to guide them, bless them, encourage them, and keep them safe.

At times in our lives, we all have strained relationships, we all make mistakes, we all have disagreements and regrets. Prayer is the best place to begin breathing life into a strained relationship. Ask God for wisdom in how to repair strained relationships and search the Scriptures and seek counsel on what you can do to reconcile the relationship.

We Breathe Life by Encouraging

The word "encourage" means to give or increase confidence to inspire with courage. I often talk to people who are discouraged and struggling with the challenges of life. Simply expressing confidence, hope, and interest in another human can often make an amazing difference in their spirit. Anyone can breathe life into others by encouraging them. This can be accomplished by simple things such as a written note, a spoken word of encouragement, or a warm embrace.

We Breathe Life by Sharing Our Journey

Sometimes we can breathe life into our loved one by taking the time to share a cup of coffee, going on a drive together, or pulling up a chair and having a heart-to-heart conversation. I have found that taking the time to talk with someone who is struggling and to share some of my own goals and struggles with them is helpful. There have been occasions when I would ask people for advice on a project I was working on. Involving them in my journey often breathed life into their own dreams.

We Breathe Life by Sharing a Life Lesson

Whenever I come across a passage of Scripture or inspiration from any other source that speaks to my heart or encourages me in a special way, I will often share it with my loved ones. If the passage inspires me or helps me with a challenge, chances are it will also help those I love. Anytime you learn a life lesson that helps you, try sharing it with those who are traveling the journey of life with you.

We Breathe Life by Our Example

We certainly learn from our own life experiences, but we also learn valuable lessons from observing how other people endure their struggles. We can breathe life into others by being an example of perseverance, faith in God, and by treating those who want to harm us with love and forgiveness.

My friend Dr. Tom Wallace is nearly ninety years old, and he is still going strong. He has had his share of challenges and disappointments in life, but he keeps on going. He continues to minister in America and abroad, and he continues to write books and counsel countless ministers every week. His example of ministry and perseverance breathes life into my own journey.

We Breathe Life by Being a Witness for Christ

Not everyone has a personal relationship with Jesus Christ. As believers it is our responsibility to tell others that Jesus Christ loves them and desires a relationship with them. By doing so, we are offering them the opportunity to have new life breathed into them by God Himself. In John 5:24, Jesus said, *"Verily, verily, I say unto you, He that heareth My word, and believeth on Him that sent Me, hath everlasting life, and shall not come into condemnation; but is passed from death unto life."* When we believe on Jesus Christ as our personal Saviour, the Holy Spirit comes to abide in us. His presence in our spirit brings new life and everlasting life. Romans 8:16 says, *"The Spirit itself beareth witness with our spirit, that we are the children of God."*

As you come into contact with your loved ones today, ask yourself, how can I breathe life into their spirit?

CHAPTER 9
The Voice Principle

One of the most valuable lessons I've learned about relationships was taught to me by a teenage girl named Erin. This beautiful young lady came to live with Debbie and me for a year because she continued to have struggles in what had been a very tumultuous life. Erin never had a secure home until she was sixteen, and she struggled to adapt to being in a secure environment. She had lived with relatives, had been in foster care, was emotionally unstable, and was very, very angry at the world.

One particular day, Erin was having what I refer to as a meltdown. We sat in our family room and I let Erin scream as loud as she could. The anger that had been bottled up for a long time was finally surfacing, and she was telling me about everything and everyone she was angry at. For more than forty-five minutes, Erin spoke from her heart. She cried and told me some of the horrible things that had happened in her life, the emotional wounds she had, the pain that was in her heart. Some of these emotions had not been expressed in sixteen years, and her anger and pain were obvious in her words, in the expression of those words, and in the tone of her voice.

Finally, after she came to a point of physical and emotional exhaustion, she stopped and looked at me with an expression of rage. With tears streaming down her face and with an angry and seemingly hopeless tone in her voice, she asked, "Aren't you going to say anything?" With tears in my own eyes I answered, "No Erin, I think you need to say something though—I'm listening."

She broke down and wept uncontrollably. Through her tears she spoke a tragic truth, "No one has ever listened to me before." No one had ever really given Erin a voice, and no one had taken the time to let Erin speak in a way that she knew she was being heard.

Often, we talk to each other, but we don't hear each other. I have found that God is a good listener, that God gives us voice. We see a beautiful example of God being a good listener in Scripture after Adam and the Woman ate of the forbidden tree. After they went into hiding and covered themselves with fig leaves, God calls out to them, *"Where art thou?"* (Genesis 3:9.) After God asked this question, He remained silent. God waited for Adam to speak, and when Adam spoke God listened. You can read every recorded account in Scripture of man speaking to God, and you will find that God always listens and never interrupts.

The Voice in the Garden

Notice that God did not call out in a condemning voice, but He called in a soft and tender voice that drew Adam and the Woman out of hiding. I can imagine that Adam and the Woman detected a certain tone in God's voice that day. Perhaps it was the tone of disappointment and the tone of sadness over the trespass that had now brought pain into the relationship. I also believe it was a voice that desired reconciliation and restoration. The voice was merciful, compassionate and forgiving.

Adam and the Woman recognized the voice because they knew God. They had communicated before. Every Christian should know the voice of God. Jesus said, *"My sheep hear my voice, and I know them, and they follow me"* (John 10:27). We should know God in such a way to know His voice. Just as a loving mother and father know the voice of their children, God also knows the voice of His children. God listens to us when we speak, and we should listen to His voice as well.

Tone of Voice

By a person's tone of the voice, we can tell if they are happy or sad, stressed or depressed, hopeful or optimistic, and we can tell that a person desires to be heard. That day in our family room, the valuable lesson I learned from Erin is one I wish I had learned long ago: everyone wants to be heard and everyone has a voice.

Could you tell me what your loved one's voice sounds like? Could you tell me what the last conversation you had with them was about? Could you tell me anything about their emotional state from the tone of their voice?

The first four letters to the word HEART spell H-E-A-R! Perhaps this is a reminder that we should hear each other with our heart. We should give those whom we love a voice, let them be heard, and listen for what is not being said.

A word of encouragement: If you have children or work with young people, give them a voice, they long to be heard.

CHAPTER 10

Time is the Communication of Love

As I write these words, I'm approaching the age of sixty, and I've come to realize that I have more time on earth to look back on than I have to look forward to. Looking back on my youth, to meeting my wife Debbie, to the births of our children—all of these events seem like they happened just a few days ago, but the reality is that all of these events transpired over the past forty years. Where has the time gone? How much of that time was wasted and how much of it was invested on life's truly important matters?

More than ever, I realize how precious a gift time really is. James was right when he asked, *"For what is your life? It is even a vapour, that appeareth for a little time, and then vanisheth away"* (James 4:14).

Time is a Gift

Genesis 3:8 tells us that God came to the Garden of Eden to walk with Adam and the Woman in the cool of the day: *"And they heard the voice of the LORD God walking in the garden in the cool of the day: and Adam and his wife hid themselves from the presence of the LORD God amongst the trees of the garden."*

Some Bible commentators conclude that the "cool of the day" refers to the early morning, others view it as the evening time. Though what time the "cool of the day" is may vary among theologians, one thing they all agree on is that God came down every day into the garden to invest in His relationship with the first humans.

There are many examples in Scripture of God investing time with humanity. In the Old Testament, God invested time with Noah, explaining who He was and how He would use Noah and his family to preserve life on earth. God invested time walking with Abraham, explaining to Abraham who He was and what He would do in Abraham's life. God spent time with Moses, explaining to him about who He was and of the important assignment God had planned for his life.

There are also New Testament examples on this principle of time being a communication of love. The primary example is Jesus leaving the presence of His Father in Heaven to come down to earth and invest thirty-three-and-a-half years with humanity. He interacted with the people, connecting with them, listening to them, and healing them.

Jesus invested time in His Apostles before and after the Resurrection. These were men He personally chose to proclaim the Gospel message of redemption and of the personal relationship with God available through Jesus Christ and to teach others to do the same. Jesus continually conversed, taught, served and relaxed with His disciples. He also invested time with His friends Mary, Martha, and Lazarus. And one of my personal favorites, Jesus invested time with children.

In Matthew 18:5, Jesus stated, *"And whoso shall receive one such little child in my name receiveth me."* Jesus not only expressed this principle that time is the communication of love, but He also demonstrated this principle in the way He lived.

The Value of the Communication of Love

I once read a powerful story that illustrates that time is the communication of love. The story is of a man who once again came home from work late to find his five-year-old son waiting for him at the door.

"Daddy, may I ask you a question?

"Yeah, sure, what is it?" the father replied.

"Daddy, how much money do you make an hour?"

"That's none of your business!" the man said angrily. "What makes you ask such a thing?"

"I just want to know. Please tell me," the little boy pleaded.

"If you must know, I make twenty dollars an hour."

"Oh," the little boy replied, bowing his head. Then looking up, he said, "Daddy, may I borrow ten dollars please?"

The father was furious. "If the only reason you wanted to know how much money I make is just so you can borrow some to buy a silly toy or some other nonsense, then you march yourself straight to your room and go to bed. I work long, hard hours every day and don't have time for such childish games."

The little boy quietly went to his room and shut the door.

The man sat down. How dare his son ask such questions only to get some money! After an hour or so, the man calmed down and started to think he may have been a little hard on his son. He didn't ask for money very often. Maybe there was something he really needed to buy. The man went to the door of the little boy's room and opened the door.

"Are you asleep, son?" he asked.

"No, Daddy, I'm awake," the boy replied.

"I've been thinking, maybe I was too hard on you earlier," the man said. "It's been a long day and I took my aggravation out on you. Here's that ten dollars you asked for."

The little boy sat straight up and beamed. "Oh, thank you, Daddy!" Then, reaching under his pillow, he pulled out some more crumpled up bills. The man, seeing the boy already had money, started to grow angry again.

The little boy slowly counted out his money then looked up at his father.

"Why did you want more money if you already had some?" the father grumbled.

"Daddy, I have twenty dollars now. Can I buy an hour of your time? Please come home early tomorrow. I would like to have dinner with you."

I can't help but wonder how often this has happened. When my children were young and really needed me, I was so busy building my career that I neglected building a relationship with them. I neglected the value of using time as a communication of love.

I thought that the best way to connect and build a relationship with them was to have a big event a couple times each year. Thankfully, my wife was always telling me that it was the day-to-day interactions that build relationships and it was the day-to-day affirmations and communication that they needed from me. My biggest regret is that I wish I would have listened better. Expensive gifts did not capture the hearts of my family. My success did not communicate my love to them. None of those things communicated my love to them the way time and positive interactions with them would have.

American businessman and author Harvey Mackay said in his book *Swim with the Sharks without Being Eaten Alive,* "Time is free, but it's priceless. You can't own it, but you can use it. You can't keep it, but you can spend it. Once you've lost it you can never get it back." That great philosopher known only as Anonymous wisely said, "The greatest gift you can give someone is your time because when you give your time, you are giving a portion of your life that you will never get back."

My friend Matt Swiatkowski shared with me that he advises people to never miss what they can never do again. If you miss your child's fifth birthday, you can never attend their fifth birthday again. I missed too many of my children's special events, but I do have a fond memory of my wife calling me at work one day to tell me that my son John, who was about four and a half years old at the time, was riding a two-wheel bicycle. Without anyone teaching him, John had climbed on the bike and coasted down a small hill in our backyard. Thankfully, I was able to go home, and for over an hour, I stood in the back yard watching my proud son ride up and down our driveway on his bicycle. To this day, I am thankful that I left work for an hour to witness John's great achievement!

I also can remember times I would pull up in the driveway, and my children would come running out of the house to greet me. By waiting on me and running out to the car to greet me, they were communicating their love to me. Oh, how I would love to return to that time and place when they were three and four and five years old. I would give them more of that precious gift of time, and I would make a more sincere effort to communicate my love to them.

Know What's Important to Those You Love

A few years ago, I jotted down a little saying, "When I was a boy my dad took me fishing. He never liked to fish, but I sure loved to go fishing. When I was a boy my dad took me fishing." The point is that what's important to our children, grandchildren, spouse, or close friends may not be important to us, but investing time doing what is important to the person we love is a way of communicating love to them. I missed too many events that were important to my children and other loved ones because I selfishly viewed the activity as not important enough for my time. I missed that it was not about the activity, but it was about showing that person love.

Thankfully, I do have good memories. One evening, my four-year-old daughter Jennifer was playing with her Barbie dolls on the floor of our family room. She asked, "Daddy, play Barbie doll with me?" I'm not all that fond of Barbie dolls, but I loved my little girl, so I sat on the floor with and played "Barbie doll."

Another fond memory that we still laugh about is playing "Beauty Salon." It was a cold winter day, and the girls were styling their hair when they decided to style my hair. They took their little hair berets and a hairbrush and began to arrange berets in my hair. When they were finished, I must have had twenty little hair berets in my hair. They laughed and thought it was a great accomplishment and wouldn't allow me to take the berets out the rest of the day! It was fun, and it didn't cost anything but that priceless commodity we call time.

Today

As long as our loved ones are still among us, it is never too late to make a memory. Most of us don't remember the exact date we did something special with someone we love, but we do remember the event and the communication of love that was expressed to us.

We cannot change the past, but we have today! Today, you can play "Hair Salon." Today, you can go rock climbing with your son. Today, you can go for a drive in the country. Today, you can send a note to say, "I'm thinking of you and I love you!" Today, you can pull up a chair and have a conversation. Today, you can use the gift of time to communicate love.

CHAPTER 11

The Value of the Person

If I offered to give you a one-hundred-dollar bill, you would probably accept it. If after offering it to you, I wadded it up like trash paper, you would probably still be willing to accept it. If I then threw the bill into the trash can, you would probably still be willing to accept it. Most of us would even be willing to reach into the trash and take it out. Why would we still want the one-hundred-dollar bill after it had been thrown into the trash? Because throwing a one-hundred-dollar bill in the trash does not decrease its value— it is still worth one hundred dollars!

In Genesis 3:6–7, we read of Adam and the Woman eating the fruit of the forbidden tree in disobedience and rebellion toward God, and we read the results of that disobedience. *"And when the woman saw that the tree was good for food, and that it was pleasant to the eyes, and a tree to be desired to make one wise, she took of the fruit thereof, and did eat, and gave also unto her husband with her; and he did eat. And the eyes of them both were opened, and they knew that they were naked; and they sewed fig leaves together, and made themselves aprons."*

In Genesis 3:8–9, we read the beginning of God's response to their disobedience. *"And they heard the voice of the LORD God walking in the garden in the cool of the day: and Adam and his wife hid themselves from the presence of the LORD God amongst the trees of the garden. And the LORD God called unto Adam, and said unto him, Where art thou?"*

Consider times in the past when someone hurt you with their words or actions. How did you respond? Our first response is usually to say that we will never have anything to do with them and we will never trust them again. When Adam and the Woman went against God's command, God could have written them off, He could have severed the relationship and just let them die. Instead, God acted in love, compassion, reconciliation, and restoration.

When Adam and the Woman realized what had happened, they went into hiding and made aprons of fig leaves to cover themselves, evidence that they knew they had disobeyed God. Despite their trespass, God reached out to Adam and the Woman and initiated reconciliation.

Now here is the question, why did God come to them after they had committed such a grievance against Him? Why would God reach out to man after man had wasted all that God had done for him?

The answer is this, God valued them! He valued each person, and He valued the relationship He had with them. Adam and the Woman were more important to God than the wrong they had done. Because the people God created were so important to Him, He was willing to come to them for reconciliation; He did not wait for them to come to Him!

Too often we throw people away because they have done something wrong, they have embarrassed us, or they have trespassed against us by their words and deeds. We overlook the value and potential of the person and the relationship. Sometimes we even throw away everything we have invested in the relationship.

May I offer another example from the Scriptures about seeking to restore and reconcile with those who waste their own lives, hurt us, or waste our relationship with them? The story of the prodigal son and his father is an amazing example of mercy and restoration. The word prodigal means "waster or one who wastes."

In the story, the prodigal son takes his inheritance from his father, goes to a far country, and wastes all of his inheritance on unlawful living. After his money was gone, his friends abandoned him, and he was at the point of starvation, the prodigal son decided he would return to his father's house, ask forgiveness, and offer to serve as a hired employee. When the son returned home, the father welcomed him with open arms, falling on his neck and kissing him then calling for a celebration because his son had returned.

The father did not disown his son, and he did not refuse him when he returned home. The son had repented of his trespass, returned home in humility, and confessed his wrong behavior. While the son had wasted all of his inheritance, the father saw the value of the son as more important than the wasted inheritance.

We must not overlook the value of the person or the potential they have when they do wrong. We must seek to reconcile and restore the person, because the person has value.

Do you know someone that needs reconciliation? Follow God's example, and reach out to them, see their value. Just because someone has been thrown away or has thrown themselves away, does not mean their value has decreased.

CHAPTER 12

The First Word Spoken

We have seen the comedy shows where the husband walks into the kitchen for his breakfast and berates his wife, "Edith, if you don't trim your toenails today, you will have to sleep on the floor tonight." Well, it's possible that Edith needs to trim her toenails, but that is not the way to greet your spouse the first thing in the morning. The first words we speak when we greet our loved ones should not be a complaint, criticism, or reprimand, but should be words of endearment, encouragement, and edification.

This principle I call "the first word spoken" can improve any relationship, and is a simple principle to apply to our lives. The Scriptures tell us God created the world with His spoken word. Consider how much our corner of the world we create by the words we speak and the actions that follow. And consider how much our words affect our relationships and the people in our lives.

In Genesis 1:28–30, we find the first recorded words God spoke to man, *"And God blessed them, and God said unto them, Be fruitful, and multiply, and replenish the earth, and subdue it: and have dominion over the fish of the sea, and over the fowl of the air, and over every living thing that moveth upon the earth. And God said, Behold, I have given you every herb bearing seed, which is upon the face of all the earth, and every tree, in the which is the fruit of a tree yielding seed; to you it shall be for meat. And to every beast of the earth, and to every fowl of the air, and to every thing that creepeth upon the earth, wherein there is life, I have given every green herb for meat: and it was so."*

These are the first recorded words of God speaking to man. In Genesis 2, we have more information about the first words God spoke to man after He breathed into Adam and made him a living soul. Genesis 2:7 says, *"And the LORD God formed man of the dust of the ground, and breathed into his nostrils the breath of life; and man became a living soul."* In Genesis 2:15–17, we read these words spoken by God to man, *"And the LORD God took the man, and put him into the Garden of Eden to dress it and to keep it. And the LORD God commanded the man, saying, Of every tree of the garden thou mayest freely eat: But of the tree of the knowledge of good and evil, thou shalt not eat of it: for in the day that thou eatest thereof thou shalt surely die."*

The first words God spoke to man were significant, they laid the foundation for Adam's life and the liberty and opportunity he had in the garden and in his relationship with God. We can change the direction of a total stranger's day with the words we speak to them, and we can instill confidence in those we daily interact with, beginning with the first words we speak to them each day of their lives. Proverbs 10:11 reminds us that our words have power, *"The mouth of a righteous man is a well of life: but violence covereth the mouth of the wicked."* And Proverbs 18:21 says, *"Death and life are in the power of the tongue . . . "* Our words should speak life. Let's learn from the following examples of some of God's first spoken words to man:

"Of every tree of the Garden thou mayest freely eat . . . "

God is telling man, "This is all for you. This garden is an expression of my love for you. This is our place of fellowship, and this is where I will commune with you." The garden was a sacred place. It was the place where God would meet with man, and it was a place of nurturing.

My wife Debbie and I had an eighteen-year-old young lady come to live with us for a year. I will call her Elizabeth. This young woman had grown up in an abusive home and had a very difficult childhood. She knew when she came to live with us that her situation was going to be different. We were not part of the foster care program; we were not receiving any monetary compensation for having her in our home. We simply desired to show her unconditional Christian love.

On the day Elizabeth arrived, we gave her a tour. I took her into the kitchen and showed her where everything was. I said, "Elizabeth, this is your kitchen; everything in here is for you. The food in the pantry and refrigerator is your food." I took her to our family room and said, "This is your family room, and that is your television. You may enjoy this room as you like." When I showed Elizabeth her bedroom, I said, "Elizabeth, this is your room. You may decorate it as you like. We only ask that you keep it clean."

In God's relationship with Adam, the first conversation He had with Adam was to explain that He had created a place for him to live; thus, in my conversation with Elizabeth, my desire was to give her ownership, to encourage her that we wanted to be part of her life, and to show her that we had invited her into our home to commune with her. I began this process with the words I spoke to her.

> *"This is now bone of my bones, and flesh of my flesh: she shall be called Woman, because she was taken out of Man."*

These are the first recorded words spoken by Adam to the Woman. These are words of edification and confirmation. Why would a man begin his day by speaking words of criticism or hostility to his wife? Why would a wife do the same to her husband? And why would we speak words of criticism and wrath to our children when we could sow hop and nurture love and affection with our words?

When Elizabeth came to live with us, we knew that she was battling depression and other emotional challenges, so we decided to do all we could to encourage her. Each morning when Elizabeth would come out of her room, I would greet her with, "Good morning, Princess, how are you this morning?" At first, she just looked at me like I was strange.

One morning when Elizabeth was really struggling, she came out of her room, and I greeted her with my usual "Good morning, Princess, how are you this morning?" She stopped, looked at me for a moment, then returned to her room. A few moments later she came back out, and I greeted her again. This time, she looked at me a moment longer then returned to her room again. After a few minutes, she came back out, and I once again greeted her with, "Good morning, Princess, how are you this morning?" Then I asked if something was wrong, because each time I greeted her she would return to her room. Tears began to stream down her face, and she said, "I just wanted to hear you call me Princess again and ask me how I am. No one has ever spoken so kindly to me or been so happy to see me."

It did not take any special effort to greet Elizabeth with words that gave her some encouragement and to confirm that she was special to Debbie and me and to make sure that the first words she heard for the day were words of love and affection.

Speak Words of Blessing

In Numbers 6:24–26, we find that God had instructed Moses to speak these word to the children of Israel, *"The LORD bless thee, and keep thee: The LORD make His face shine upon thee, and be gracious unto thee: The LORD lift up His countenance upon thee, and give thee peace."*

Take advantage of opportunities to speak the Scriptures to your loved ones. We can do this by sharing a passage that has been a blessing to us, by leaving a note with a Bible verse on it, or by texting an encouraging Bible verse. A friend's wife used to put handwritten Bible verses and words of affection in my friend's luggage when he went on a trip. The Bible has power so use Scripture to speak words of blessing to those you love.

Answer with Soft Words

Sometimes the first words we respond with cause a problem. Proverbs 15:1 tells us, *"A soft answer turneth away wrath: but grievous words stir up anger."*

The word "soft" has the meaning of gentle, mild, tender, and courteous. If someone is having a bad day, answering with words that stir up anger will only add fuel to a fire. If we respond with soft answers, we can often turn the conversation in a better direction.

It is important to act upon what will bring about a good outcome and not react to the anger, pain, or confusion a person is unleashing on you.

We Write on the Heart with Our Spoken Words

Second Corinthians 3:2–3 says, *"Ye are our epistle* (letter) *written in our hearts, known and read of all men: Forasmuch as ye are manifestly declared to be the epistle of Christ ministered by us, written not with ink, but with the Spirit of the living God; not in tables of stone, but in fleshy tables of the heart."*

The words we speak can leave lasting memories upon the human heart, especially for those who are closest to us because they desire our words of love the most. If we tell someone that they have value, that they are loved, and that their life has great purpose, we are doing more than just speaking words; we are engraving hope, acceptance, confidence, and assurance upon the tablet of their heart that will give them strength to persevere when difficulties come.

For much of her childhood, Elizabeth was told she was nothing. As she was passed from family member to family member to stranger, she was made to feel unwanted. One family even told her that she was just a paycheck to them. Thankfully, not all foster parents are like that! Words that were spoken to her had wounded Elizabeth's spirit. By using kind words, we were able to see healing and growth in Elizabeth, and we are very proud of her.

Our Words Come from Our Heart

Jesus said, *"For out of the abundance of the heart the mouth speaketh"* (Matthew 12:34b). When we greet those we love and cherish, we must make certain that we don't have any anger, bitterness, or malice in our heart. We need to see our loved one as a gift God has placed into our life to love, nurture, and influence.

If we have unresolved issues in our relationship with them, then it is time to speak about the things that are unresolved to find reconciliation.

What were the last "first words" you spoke to those closest to you? Were they words of encouragement, edification, and love?

CHAPTER 13

Good Relationships Are Intentional

God was intentional in creating the world, He was also intentional when He created man, and He is intentional in His relationship with us. We see this truth very clearly in the following passage, *"And God said, Let Us make man in Our image, after Our likeness: and let them have dominion over the fish of the sea, and over the fowl of the air, and over the cattle, and over all the earth, and over every creeping thing that creepeth upon the earth. So God created man in His own image, in the image of God created He him; male and female created He them. And God blessed them, and God said unto them, Be fruitful, and multiply, and replenish the earth, and subdue it: and have dominion over the fish of the sea, and over the fowl of the air, and over every living thing that moveth upon the earth. And God said, Behold, I have given you every herb bearing seed, which is upon the face of all the earth, and every tree, in the which is the fruit of a tree yielding seed; to you it shall be for meat"* (Genesis 1:26–29).

If we are going to have the best relationships possible, we must be intentional in making them the best they can possibly be. Let's examine how we can make our relationships intentionally good.

Purpose of Relationships

Every relationship has a purpose but not all relationships have the same purpose. The relationship I have with my wife is different than the relationship I have with any other human being. Marriage is the only relationship God instituted where two people become one. The primary purpose of the marriage relationship is for companionship. Before God created woman, He said, *"It is not good that the man should be alone . . . "* (Genesis 2:18).

The purpose of friendship is also for companionship and is the bonding agent for all other relationships. We have business relationships that serve their own purpose. The relationships we form with like-minded believers are also special for unique reasons, we have a common bond in Christ, we have a family like connection as children of God and we have a common purpose in our worship and propagation of the Gospel message.

Common Bonds of Relationships

Scripture tells us in 2 Corinthians 6:14, *"Be ye not unequally yoked together with unbelievers: for what fellowship hath righteousness with unrighteousness? and what communion hath light with darkness?"*

The common bond of a relationship can sometimes be a challenge. For example, anger, bitterness, rebellion, and other negative emotions can be common bonds in a relationship; however, negative feeds upon negative and positive feeds upon positive in a relationship. The common bond of our closest relationships should first be Jesus Christ, followed by serving God, serving others, and edifying one another.

Recognition of Differences in Relationships

Our relationships are different with different people as no two people are the same. I have a dear friend named Joe, whom I have been friends with for nearly fifty years. Joe has his own unique personality, and we have more than one common bond. I also have a friend named Tom, whom I have been friends with for forty over years. Joe and Tom have different personalities and interests, and our common bonds are a little different. Joe is active in his church, is married, is retired from the military, and his favorite pastime is a good game of golf. Tom does not attend church, is single, is a supervisor with a construction company, and his favorite pastime is to take a long ride on his Harley Davidson motorcycle or classic car. My common bond with these two men is that we grew up together; Tom and I worked at the same fast food restaurant during high school, while Joe and I grew up in the same church. I have spent many hours with both of these friends at different times. We helped each other through the struggles of our teen years, and we helped each other with important decisions. The point is God made us different, and we should recognize the differences and enjoy people for who they are and for the connection we have to them.

Strengthening Relationships

"Iron sharpeneth iron; so a man sharpeneth the countenance of his friend" (Proverbs 27:17). When any relationship has the purpose of intentionally strengthening the other, that relationship will be productive for all parties. When a marriage is intentionally strong and thriving, the children are going to thrive. When church leaders and the congregation are intentionally strong, the community will thrive. When an employer and employees are intentionally strong, the business will thrive.

If you truly want to improve your relationships, you will need to make an earnest effort on your part. When all parties involved want to make improvements and are willing to be intentional, great things can happen!

CHAPTER 14

Good Relationships Require Sacrifices

In an episode of the comic strip "Peanuts," Charlie Brown cracks open his piggy bank. He says to Lucy, "Look, I've got $9.11 to spend on Christmas gifts."

Lucy is not impressed as she says, "You can't buy something for everyone with $9.11, Charlie Brown."

Charlie Brown says, "Oh yeah? Well I'm gonna try!"

"Then," Lucy continues, "they're sure gonna be cheap presents."

Charlie says with absolute conviction, "Nothing is cheap if it costs all that you have."

People often say they want their relationships to improve, but they are unwilling to take the necessary steps or make sacrifices to improve them.

Genesis 3:21 says, *"Unto Adam also and to his wife did the LORD God make coats of skins, and clothed them."* This short verse reveals an important relationship principle as these words introduce the model in which God teaches us to seek reconciliation and restoration in our relationships. Although the word sacrifice is not used in the verse, God's actions demonstrate sacrifice. The word "sacrifice" means, to destroy, surrender, or suffer to be lost for the sake of obtaining something. Let's evaluate the sacrifice God made for Adam and Eve's coverings to see what we can learn about relationships.

God Went to Them

After their sin, Adam and Eve made aprons of fig leaves and went into hiding. They were no doubt ashamed of what they had done, but despite their shame, they did not go to God seeking forgiveness or reconciliation with Him. However, we do find a loving and merciful God coming to Adam and the Woman. God had not wronged them, God had not sinned against Adam and the Woman, God had not breached His relationship with them, yet He is the one that reached out to them in reconciliation.

God Offered the Sacrifice

Adam and the Woman did not make the sacrifice, God did. Adam and the Woman had never seen bloodshed. They had never witnessed death. Imagine how traumatic it would have been for Adam and the Woman to witness God take the life of an innocent animal and make coats of skins to cover them with. Sometimes to reconcile our relationships with others, we must make a difficult sacrifice.

The Sacrifice Demonstrates the Value of the One Sacrificed for

When God offered a sacrifice to cover Adam and the Woman, He expressed to them that He deemed them valuable and that He valued His relationship with them. When we make sacrifices to improve our relationships or to restore broken relationships, our sacrifices express to the other party that we value them and our relationship with them.

The Reconciliation was about Adam and the Woman

We often think reconciling with someone is about us. We've been wronged, we won't forgive, and we won't seek reconciliation because the reconciliation about us, but it's not about you!

Ultimately, everything is about the glory of God, but we must understand this; Jesus did not shed his blood and die on the cross for His sin. He shed His blood on the cross and died for our sin. In this sense, the cross is about us.

When God the Father made a sacrifice to cover Adam and the Woman, God had not sinned against them, God had not offended them, and God had not wronged them! In that sense, the sacrifice was not about God, it was about Adam and the Woman. It was about their reconciliation to God.

God Completely Covered Adam and the Woman

When you make a sacrifice in reconciliation, you don't continually bring up the wrong. If you do continue to hold that grudge, you have not truly come to terms that someone has wronged you, and you have not truly sacrificed something to make it right.

God made a sacrifice for you and me to be forgiven, reconciled, restored, and redeemed. When you are willing to sacrifice for reconciliation, you will find it possible to reconcile to someone.

Sometimes Sacrifices Are Necessary

When the Hoover Dam was built, it was the largest dam in the world. As is common on such projects, there were the inevitable accidents and some workmen lost their lives. When the dam was complete, they put a plaque on the wall and inscribed the names of the workmen who had died during construction on it. The plaque begins, "These died that the desert might rejoice and blossom as the rose."

The building of the Hoover Dam was important, and the loss of life was tragic, but without those sacrifices, the dam would not have been completed. Sometimes sacrifices are necessary for reconciliation and restoration. As difficult as sacrifices can be, we must realize that in the end our relationships can be restored, lives can be redeemed, and that which was a desert can blossom as the rose.

CHAPTER 15

Our Four Human Needs

When I was twenty-seven, I attended a two-week class for sales associates with the company I was working for. In one of the lessons on the psychology of sales, the instructor shared why people make large purchases, why they will spend money on things for themselves, and why they are often willing to go into debt for material things. He wrote on the chalkboard the four needs we all have:

I need someone to love me

I need to feel important

I need hope

I want to live (or I need my life to have purpose)

I was writing all of this down, when Pat, the man sitting next to me who was also a Christian, leaned over and said, "That's John 3:16. *'For God so loved the world,* (I am loved) *that He gave His only begotten son* (I am important), *that whosoever believeth in Him should not perish* (I have hope), *but have everlasting life* (I live forever).'"

Over the years I have taught on what I now call the four human needs. There are three areas in our relationships where this teaching will help us. The first area is that we all seek people who will fulfill these four human needs because we all want to be loved, we all want to feel that we are important, we all want hope, and we all want to believe that our life has meaning.

Secondly, everyone you know has these same four human needs. Most people try to fulfill their own human needs and give little thought to fulfilling the human needs of others. We think other people should make us happy, especially those with whom we have our closest relationships, but there is more fulfillment in helping others fulfill their four human needs than seeking our own fulfillment.

Thirdly, my friend Pat was right, the four human needs are outlined in John 3:16. Every human need you and I and everyone else have is fulfilled in the person of Jesus Christ. If you don't have a relationship with him, He invites you to believe on Him.

Meditate on the four human needs and seek to fulfill them in the lives of your loved ones. In your relationship with those closest to you ask yourself, do they feel loved by me? Do I make them feel important? Do I give them hope or am I disappointing them? Do I add to their life purpose?

I challenge you, the next time you meet a total stranger, treat them in a way that they feel loved, important, hopeful, and purposeful. Do this and you may gain a new friend.

CHAPTER 16

Trespasses

Remember the story of the porcupines? They were cold, so they huddled together, but they jabbed each other with their quills. Sometimes we jab someone in a relationship or cross a boundary—this is called trespassing against someone. A trespass is defined as an injury or offense done to another, to pass over the boundary line of another.

To improve our relationships, there are many positive actions that we should add to our lives as we have suggested already. There are also things we must learn to refrain from doing. The reality is that we all trespass against those we are close to. We sometimes do this without even knowing it.

I recall a time Debbie and I were in the checkout line at the grocery store. Without thinking, I asked her a question that was out of place. Tears filled her eyes, and when we reached the car, she told me that the question had hurt her. I had no intention of hurting her, but I had trespassed against her. I immediately apologized and asked for her forgiveness, assuring her that the question came out wrong and was not meant to be hurtful. Debbie graciously accepted my apology and forgave me. I was reminded once again that the best apology is a change in behavior.

We all trespass against others. Jesus knew we would trespass and taught His disciples to pray accordingly. Matthew 6:9–14 says, *"After this manner therefore pray ye: Our Father which art in heaven, hallowed be Thy name. Thy kingdom come, Thy will be done in earth, as it is in heaven. Give us this day our daily bread. And forgive us our debts, as we forgive our debtors. And lead us not into temptation, but deliver us from evil: For Thine is the kingdom, and the power, and the glory, for ever. Amen. For if ye forgive men their trespasses, your heavenly Father will also forgive you."*

We trespass against our spouse, our children, our parents, our friends, our acquaintances, and against strangers. We can trespass by our actions, by lack of action, and by our words. Knowing how to deal purposefully with our trespasses will help us in our relationships.

Jesus' Teaching on Trespasses

"Take heed to yourselves: If thy brother trespass against thee, rebuke him; and if he repent, forgive him. And if he trespass against thee seven times in a day, and seven times in a day turn again to thee, saying, I repent; thou shalt forgive him" (Luke 17:3–4).

Jesus begins with the instruction to *"Take heed to yourselves . . . "* He is telling us to pay attention to how we treat each other and be intentional and purposeful in how we respond when we are trespassed against. Our behavior and treatment of people will affect those we have a relationship with. Our desired outcome should be to have positive results; thus, we must be intentional in our relationships and take heed to the words we speak, the actions we take, and the activities we engage in.

We must also take heed that we do not involve ourselves with the wrong people in the first place. Evildoers can influence us to go against our convictions and against those who truly do love us and have our best interest at heart. For example, the Woman paid a high price for interacting with the Serpent. To avoid being influenced toward evil, we should avoid the wrong people whenever possible.

Jesus' Instruction on Responding to Trespasses

Notice His teaching in Luke 17:3, *"If thy brother trespass against thee . . ."* The key word here is brother—Jesus is talking to believers. We usually deal differently with fellow believers than we do unbelievers since Christians have a common bond in our mutual relationship with Jesus Christ. Jesus is teaching here that our response to our brothers and sisters in the family of God should have a more positive outcome than we might get with an unbeliever because we hold the same values and beliefs about forgiveness and restoration.

Jesus instructs believers, *"If thy brother trespass against thee, rebuke him . . . "* It has been my experience that we often misunderstand the word rebuke, thinking it means to confront harshly and with anger. To rebuke actually means to correct, to prevent from going the wrong way. Do we sometimes need to be stern in our rebuke? Yes, but the point of a rebuke is to keep someone from going the wrong way.

Debbie and I recently went to watch our little granddaughters Alayna and Aleah cheerlead at a children's tag football game. Watching them cheer on the young athletes was fun and entertaining as well as a learning experience. One little boy got the football several times, and each time he took off running in any direction. Each time he ran the wrong way, one of the coaches or one of the referees would take hold of his shoulders and turn him in the right direction. They did not stop him, they did not lecture him, they did not speak in anger to him; instead, they guided him in the direction he needed to go. This is a good example of how we should approach someone who has trespassed against us. The purpose of rebuke is to point out the trespass, to correct the person, and to guide them to the right path.

Continuing in His teaching in Luke 17:3, Jesus says, *" . . . if he repent, forgive him."* Jesus teaches that if the one who has trespassed against us repents, our responsibility becomes to forgive the trespass and the person who committed the trespass. The Apostle Paul gives a clear description of the perspective we should have in forgiving someone who has trespassed against us. Ephesians 4:29–32 says, *"Let no corrupt communication proceed out of your mouth, but that which is good to the use of edifying, that it may minister grace unto the hearers. And grieve not the Holy Spirit of God, whereby ye are sealed unto the day of redemption.*

Let all bitterness, and wrath, and anger, and clamour, and evil speaking, be put away from you, with all malice: And be ye kind one to another, tenderhearted, forgiving one another, even as God for Christ's sake hath forgiven you."

The subject of forgiveness is worthy of an in-depth study, but I will offer the following outline:

Have a humble perspective or attitude about forgiveness.

Paul writes in Ephesians 4:2, *"With all lowliness and meekness, with longsuffering, forbearing one another in love."* Paul knew that the purpose of forgiving a trespass is to reconcile the relationship. Exemplifying this principle, Jesus died on the cross for us, so that we could be forgiven of our trespasses against God and so that our relationship with Him could be reconciled. We must then have a forgiving attitude toward the person who has trespassed against us and is now seeking our forgiveness.

Let your communication be proactive.

Paul stresses in Ephesians 4:29, *"Let no corrupt (rotten, putrefied) communication come out of your mouth . . . but that which is good to the use of edifying (build up, instruct), that it may minister grace unto the hearers."* When we are forgiving someone that has trespassed against us, we need to use this as an opportunity to build and disciple them in their personal spiritual growth rather than tear them down and hinder their personal spiritual growth.

Don't trespass against God when reconciling a trespass against you.

Paul says in Ephesians 4:30, *"And grieve not the Holy Spirit of God . . . "* When we respond toward someone who has trespassed against us by speaking corrupt things about them, we grieve God with such a reaction; therefore, we are trespassing against God by talking destructively about someone who trespassed against us.

Examine your own heart.

In Ephesians 4:31, Paul instructs, *"Let all bitterness, and wrath, and anger, and clamour* (complaining loudly), *and evil speaking, be put away from you, with all malice* (a desire in the heart to hurt)." As we enter the reconciliation process, it is crucial that we examine our own hearts before God. We must remove any deep-rooted emotions of anger, bitterness, and desires to seek vengeance. Having these emotions in check will allow us to act upon what is right rather than react in anger, hurt, or malice.

Forgive as God forgives us.

In Ephesians 4:32, Paul concludes with a reminder to believers of God's forgiveness: *"And be ye kind one to another, tenderhearted, forgiving one another, even as God for Christ's sake hath forgiven you."* Paul reminds us that God is willing to forgive us of our trespasses because He loves His Son Jesus Christ. He forgives us because Jesus willingly went to the cross to give His own body as a sacrifice, shed His blood, and die for our trespasses. Therefore, we must be willing to forgive those who trespass against us because we love Jesus Christ. Once we have followed through with rebuke, repentance, and forgiveness, our focus in the reconciliation process can turn to restoring the relationship.

Find freedom in forgiveness.

Corrie Ten Boom said in *Tramp for the Lord*, "Forgiveness is setting the prisoner free, only to find out that the prisoner was me." Some people have the idea that if we forgive someone, we are somehow helping the person who hurt us, or we think that by not forgiving them, we are keeping them in bondage. The truth is by not forgiving someone who has trespassed against us, we are keeping ourselves in bondage. Forgiveness sets ourselves free.

Continued Offenses

In Luke 17:4, Jesus addresses the issue of people continuing to trespass: *"And if he trespass against thee seven times in a day, and seven times in a day turn again to thee, saying, I repent; thou shalt forgive him."* The word repent implies that the trespasser has begged for forgiveness and changed his behavior, that he has made a sincere effort to make things right.

Forgiving Trespasses Should Be Part of Our Prayer Life

C. S. Lewis said, "To be a Christian means to forgive the inexcusable because God has forgiven the inexcusable in you" (*The Weight of Glory: And Other Addresses*). Someone may not know that they have trespassed against you. While you don't need to tell everyone, you do need to tell the Lord. In our prayer time, we should pray for the trespasser and forgive them in our heart. It is also interesting to note that in Jesus' teaching on prayer in Matthew 6:14–15, He never mentions a requirement for the trespasser to repent or to ask for forgiveness, Jesus simply instructs us to forgive. *"For if ye forgive men their trespasses, your heavenly Father will also forgive you: But if ye forgive not men their trespasses, neither will your Father forgive your trespasses."* In following Jesus' teaching, forgiving those who trespass against us is something that begins in our private prayer regardless of whether or forgiveness has been sought.

There Can Be Life after Trespasses

Relationships will decay and die without forgiveness, but they can be renewed and live on with forgiveness. Paul writes in Ephesians 2:1, *"And you hath He quickened* (made alive), *who were dead in trespasses and sins."* God brings us back to life from our trespasses through His forgiving power. By forgiving others, we too can give life to those who have trespassed against us, even if they never ask for forgiveness and never change their ways. The best way to rekindle a relationship, however, is for the trespasser to seek forgiveness, change their behavior, and receive forgiveness.

CHAPTER 17

Mending Our Mistakes

"Therefore if thou bring thy gift to the altar, and there rememberest that thy brother hath ought against thee; Leave there thy gift before the altar, and go thy way; first be reconciled to thy brother, and then come and offer thy gift."

Matthew 5:23–24

I am the father of five children, whom I love very much. Although my children are now grown and have families of their own, sometimes I look back to their childhood and wish I could have a "do-over." If I could go back in time and start over there are four things I would do differently. If you have young children, please write what I'm about to tell you on your heart.

I would strive to make sure they knew that I valued them.

Someone once wisely said, "Time is an event." If I could go back in time, I would invest more time with my children, and I would invest it more wisely and more often. It is through invested time that children believe they are valued.

I would listen better.

Anytime they came to me, I would be very careful to hear what they have to say. I would give them a voice.

I would never raise my voice to a level of "yelling."

As a parent there are times when speaking sternly is necessary, but yelling means I've lost control of myself. Yelling does not solve anything and does not edify them.

I would teach them the importance of the Bible
being the final authority in their life.

There are many philosophies to live by, but the one that has stood the test of time and is the only source that tells us of the redemption of man is the Bible.

I would teach them the importance of their relationship with God.

I grew up in a faith community that stressed outward appearance more than an inward relationship with Jesus Christ. Rules and standards are not wrong, but I've come to realize that outward appearance does not guarantee an inward relationship with Jesus. Outward appearance only means one has learned to comply with the rules of religion. I would then focus on helping my children develop their relationship with God, because it is out of that relationship that we form our convictions.

I made mistakes in the most important relationships in my life, and I have trespassed against those I love the most. Coming to realize this fact later than I should have, I have had to ask myself what steps can be taken to mend the mistakes.

Go to God first.

Having accepted the fact that you made a mistake, that you have trespassed against someone that you love, and that you have possibly wounded their spirit, you should then first pray about the matter. Confess to God that you have trespassed and ask for wisdom to mend the mistake you have made.

Use your relationship to mend your mistakes.

Someone wisely said, "Wounds caused by relationships are best healed with relationships." There are two sides to this. First, a person that has been wounded by bad or abusive relationships can be healed through loving compassionate relationships. Second, if we have caused wounds in a relationship or if we have made a mistake that has caused a breach in the relationship, taking positive actions in the relationship can mend it.

The goal is reconciliation.

To reconcile is to call back into union and friendship the affections which have been alienated; to restore to friendship or favor after estrangement. This is the goal in mending our mistakes—to return to union.

Show respect for their feelings and perspective.

By showing respect, I'm suggesting that you make an effort to relate to how they feel toward what you have done. If you are sincere in seeking reconciliation, express to those you have wronged that you see how your actions hurt or offended them.

Confess that you have made a mistake.

To confess is simply to acknowledge that you have done something wrong. Humbly go to the person you have trespassed against and confess that you were wrong. Don't try and make excuses for what you did, just confess that you realize your actions or behaviors were wrong and that you want to make things right.

Ask for forgiveness.

I have learned that it is better to ask for forgiveness than to state that you are sorry. Asking for forgiveness better relays the message that you are taking personal responsibility for your offense. It also gives the message that you realize the person does not have to forgive you but that you are putting the forgiveness decision in their hands.

Let your actions speak louder than your words.

If our mistakes have been many and if they have caused deep wounds, it will take more than asking forgiveness to truly reconcile the relationship. We will also need to change our behavior. We must be careful to not repeat our mistakes, but rather, we must change our actions and let our actions speak louder than our confession and apology.

Give them time.

We have all heard the old saying that, "Time heals all wounds." I've never believed that statement as I believe it is what we *do* over "time" that heals wounds. If our mistakes have caused deep wounds, we must give the other person time to see that we are sincere in our confession and that we want the relationship to be at its best.

We won't resolve every issue.

The goal of reconciliation is not to agree on an issue but to reconcile the relationship. No matter what we do, we are not going to agree on everything, and we are not going to see everything the same way. We are all different. However, we can seek to understand and be understood so that we can get along even when we don't agree on an issue.

Mended relationships are stronger relationships.

Ships that survive storms usually need repairs, but after the storm and after the repairs are complete, the ship is stronger than it was before because the storm revealed the ship's weaknesses and the necessary repairs made it stronger. I have learned that the same can be true of our relationships. The storms we weather through our mistakes and trespasses can reveal our weaknesses, but once we repair those weaknesses, our relationships can be stronger than ever.

We can experience better relationships and those experiences begin with improving ourselves. It is never too late to improve ourselves!

CHAPTER 18

Good Relationship
Behaviors Are Taught

Years ago, I worked with a young man by the name of David. On our first day working together, I was riding with David to an appointment when we came to a bridge. David became visibly nervous and pulled the car over to the side of the road and came to a complete stop. As this was before wearing a seat belt was mandatory, David fastened his safety belt, looked over at me, and said, "Put your seat belt on and get ready."

Out of respect, I fastened my seat belt.

By this time, perspiration was breaking out on David's brow, his face was red with fear, and he was trembling. He looked over at me again, put the car into drive, and said, "Brace yourself." I obeyed, then David asked, "Are you ready?" After my affirmative response, David looked into the rearview mirror, placed both hands firmly on the steering wheel, looked at the road ahead, and said, "Here we go!"

He floored the accelerator, and we crossed the bridge at sixty-five miles per hour. After we crossed the bridge, David pulled over to the side of the road and parked the car. He took a deep breath, leaned his head back, and closed his eyes in exhaustion.

I asked, "David, are you all right?"

"I will be in a minute." He took a deep breath. "I'm afraid of crossing bridges."

I politely responded, "Have you been in an accident on a bridge?"

David answered, "No!"

"Have you ever seen a bridge collapse or something bad happen with a bridge, like someone dying or something?"

David again answered, "No!"

In a kind and gentle tone, I said, "No offense David, but I've never met anyone that feared crossing a bridge so much."

David responded with a statement I will never forget, "If you think I'm afraid of bridges, you should meet my dad. He won't cross a bridge at all unless there is no other way around it."

David learned the fear of bridges from his father. He had never been in an accident on a bridge, he had never witnessed an accident on a bridge, and he had never seen a bridge collapse. Because he had witnessed his father's fear of bridges, however, he had learned to fear crossing bridges.

Like David learning to fear bridges from his father, most of what we practice in our relationships are things we have learned. We learn how to treat others from the way we are treated. We learn how to express love from the way love is expressed toward us. We learn how to cope with stress from the way stress is expressed toward us. A child that grows up in a home where family members yell at one another, will yell at others when life is not going his or her way. A child who grows up not being valued and who is not nurtured emotionally is not going to value themselves or others and is likely to have relationship challenges. Good or bad relationship behaviors are first taught in the home.

We Teach Others by Example

Thankfully, I did not learn the fear of bridges from David that day, but if I was a seven-year-old and had looked up to David as a mentor, I may have been convinced by David's example that I, too, should fear bridges. We can influence young people about good relationship behaviors, not by what we tell them but by what we show them through our own relationship behaviors.

I will never forget my fifth grade Sunday school teacher, Mr. Lawrence Schaffer. One Saturday, he invited each pupil in our boys' Sunday school class out to his house for a Christmas party. During the party, we played games, ate hotdogs and popcorn, and did stuff fifth grade boys do. Just imagine the conversations, "Batman is cooler than Superman because he has the cool car," or, "John Wayne is the best ever, because he shoots guns and gets to ride a horse." These were my normal topics of conversation when I was ten—very important stuff to know!

The thing I remember most about that Christmas party was the way Mr. Schaffer treated Mrs. Schaffer. He spoke politely to Mrs. Schaffer, never raising his voice, never cursing or threatening to hit her. They spoke lovingly to each other, they smiled at each other, they laughed together, and without knowing it, they taught a fifth-grade boy what a marriage relationship can be. Through their influence and example, they taught me positive relationship behaviors.

We Can Learn Good Relationship Behaviors

It is never too late to change or make improvements in our relationship behaviors. If you learned negative relationship behaviors, begin learning and practicing new ones today. Learn about yourself and begin treating people the way you would want to be treated. The golden rule can serve as our guide in all of our relationships, *"And as ye would that men should do to you, do ye also to them likewise"* (Luke 6:31).

CHAPTER 19

Changes in Our Relationships

Someone wisely said, "A true relationship is two imperfect people refusing to give up on each other." May I add to that quote, that we must especially not give up on each other when change enters our lives! Although this lesson will apply to our closet relationships, it will be helpful in all of life's relationships.

There are many reasons change comes into our relationships: a shift in circumstances, age and maturity, an illness, a trespass or betrayal, a traumatic event, or any major positive event. Change will come into your relationships, and ultimately, it will be your relationship with God, family, and close friends that will sustain you through the changes.

The following outline in Genesis 3 will help us with changes in our relationships:

Watch out for change.

Not everyone that comes into our lives or our relationships are intruders and cause problems, but the Serpent caused some major problems for Adam and the Woman. The Serpent's purpose was to bring conflict between man and God, and this is still Satan's primary activity today. After the dust settled, the Serpent had invoked major changes in the relationship between Adam and the Woman and between them and God. They ended up going into hiding and covering themselves because of their shame.

Listen for the voice of God.

Genesis 3:8 says, *"And they heard the voice of the LORD God walking in the garden in the cool of the day . . . "* When change enters our lives, it is wise to listen to the voice of God. When God spoke, Adam answered. When we are experiencing change in our relationships or when a change in our circumstances has taken place, we must listen to God's voice in our hearts and from Scripture and respond to the leadership God is giving us.

Analyze what brought about the change.

This is what God helped Adam and the Woman do in Genesis 3:9–13. *"And the LORD God called unto Adam, and said unto him, Where art thou? And he said, I heard Thy voice in the garden, and I was afraid, because I was naked; and I hid myself. And He said, Who told thee that thou wast naked? Hast thou eaten of the tree, whereof I commanded thee that thou shouldest not eat? And the man said, The woman whom Thou gavest to be with me, she gave me of the tree, and I did eat. And the LORD God said unto the woman, What is this that thou hast done? And the woman said, The serpent beguiled me, and I did eat."*

In order to make things right or to adjust to change in a relationship, we must analyze what happened and work from the point of what went wrong or from what went right.

Confront the source of change.

It is important to determine the source of change in the relationship to help with needed adjustments and to learn from the experience. When you read Genesis 3:8–13, you find that God confronted Adam and the Woman in a manner that sought restoration and reconciliation. In confronting changes that have taken place or changes that need to be made, we must confront our own reality. This is what God forced Adam and Woman to do with the questions He asked them. We must ask ourselves hard questions and confront the change.

Some Changes Bring Added Responsibilities

Changes in a relationship may put us in a position to increase our responsibilities or to increase our efforts toward improving the relationship. For example, the birth of a first child is a wonderful event in the lives of a married couple, but it also adds responsibilities to the husband and wife. The arrival of the child brings challenges that require patience and a renewal of commitment to the marriage relationship, but it also brings great blessings and an opportunity for growth in the marriage relationship.

Changes often mean that we may need to be more committed to a relationship to make improvements, to work through a difficult time, or to mend a trespass. If a teenager commits a serious trespass against his or her parents, the teenager should take personal responsibility in mending the broken trust, and both the parents and the teenager should commit to bridging any breaches in the relationship and to mending the relationship.

Some Changes Change Our Environment

After Adam and the Woman disobeyed God, He removed them from the Garden of Eden. This was a major change in their lives. The Garden of Eden was the place God had planted for the purpose of communing with the humans He created. After their disobedience and the entrance of sin into the world, Adam and the Woman could no longer commune with God in the same way, but they could still have a relationship with Him. Changes in our relationships can also bring about changes in our environment; these are usually emotional changes such as stress, grief, illness, broken trust and sorrow.

Some Changes Require Sacrifices

Genesis 3:21 tells us that God took the life of innocent animals, shed their blood, and made coverings from the skins of the animals for Adam and the Woman. This was a sacrifice necessary for the relationship to be reconciled. Sometimes positive or healing changes in our relationships require sacrifices on our part. (For more information, see Chapter 14: Good Relationships Require Sacrifices).

Changes Can Bring New Life

I find it interesting that until God confronted them about partaking of the forbidden fruit Eve's name was Woman, but in Genesis 3:20 Adam changes her name to Eve, which means breathe, living. From this point on, not only was she part of Adam, but now she would be a life giver, "the mother of all living." Perhaps this name change was a surrendering to the change that was taking place in their lives and their relationship.

Although God removed Adam and the Woman from the Garden of Eden for their disobedience, He did offer them a fresh new beginning. Genesis 4:1–2 tells us that they did give life to two sons, Cain and Abel. Unfortunately, because of their sin, Adam and the Woman were never completely free from Satan's influence, and we will never be free of it either this side of Heaven.

Certainly, the changes that took place in Adam and the Woman's lives were difficult, just as we must sometimes face difficult changes in our own relationships, but with God's help we can have a new beginning. 2 Corinthians 5:17 says, *"Therefore if any man be in Christ, he is a new creature: old things are passed away; behold, all things are become new."* That new beginning will largely depend on our perspective and desire to adjust to changes and to choose to allow the changes to make ourselves and our relationships better.

CHAPTER 20

Moving on from
Toxic Relationships

"Letting go doesn't mean giving up, but rather accepting things that cannot be."

Anonymous

I have counseled numerous people who have been repeatedly hurt in toxic relationships. I use the word toxic because it means poisonous and harmful.

Relationships are a central part of our lives. Because we are influenced by those closest to us, I want to share some principles that will help those who are struggling in a toxic relationship. We will begin by looking at the first record of a toxic relationship.

I draw your attention once again to the Garden of Eden. Genesis 3:1–6 says, *"Now the serpent was more subtil than any beast of the field which the LORD God had made. And he said unto the woman, Yea, hath God said, Ye shall not eat of every tree of the garden? And the woman said unto the serpent, We may eat of the fruit of the trees of the garden: But of the fruit of the tree which is in the midst of the garden, God hath said, Ye shall not eat of it, neither shall ye touch it, lest ye die. And the serpent said unto the woman, Ye shall not surely die: For God doth know that in the day ye eat thereof, then your eyes shall be opened, and ye shall be as gods, knowing good and evil. And when the woman saw that the tree was good for food, and that it was pleasant to the eyes, and a tree to be desired to make one wise, she*

took of the fruit thereof, and did eat, and gave also unto her husband with her; and
he did eat."

There are a couple of things that stand out in this passage, the first is that Adam and the Woman were living in a perfect environment, one that God had created for them. Secondly, we see that a toxic person, the Serpent, was able to penetrate this perfect environment and cause eternal relationship challenges. At this point, there are three people in the Woman's life, God, Adam, and the Serpent.

The Bible says that the Serpent "beguiled" the Woman. The word "beguiled" means imposed on, mislead by craft. The Serpent, who is Satan, has been beguiling people ever since man lived in the Garden of Eden. Satan is the central toxic being that influences every toxic human being you and I have ever met.

We know how this event played out. Satan lied to the Woman, tricking her into disobeying God's command. Conviction then set in and Adam and the Woman went into hiding and sewed fig leaves together to cover themselves. The curse of sin was placed on mankind. In all of this debris, we find a few lessons on handling toxic relationships.

We Must Be Honest with Ourselves

Whenever we find ourselves in a toxic relationship, we must face our own reality! After Adam and the Woman went into hiding God called out to them by asking, *"Where art thou?"* (Genesis 3:9). This is an interesting question when you consider that it is God doing the asking and He knows all things. God knew where they were, and God knew what had happened. The reason God called out to them was that God was forcing them to confront their own reality. To be honest with themselves.

In order for us to walk away from a toxic relationship, we must take the same actions that God made Adam and the Woman take. We must confront our own reality, examine the situation, then take responsibility for allowing the intruder to beguile us and stop them from influencing us. We must take our life back.

Toxic Relationships Have Lasting Effects

The Serpent's influence on Adam and the Woman had a lasting effect on their lives. Sadly, had they not allowed the Serpent to persuade them that God could not be trusted and that His word was not reliable, their lives would have been eternal bliss.

Our situations are different. Those who are toxic in our lives are not Satan disguised as a snake. They are usually just snakes. We are dealing with people, and although they are under the influence of demons, they are not demons. However, whatever influence we allow them to have in our lives can have lasting effects.

This does not mean we can't overcome these relationships and make changes in our own heart, but if we have been in toxic relationships, we should examine how they have affected us and make the necessary changes in our lives to put it behind us.

You Can Move On

It was grace, God's unmerited favor, and His undeserved love toward us that He came to Adam and the Woman after they disobeyed Him and ate of the forbidden tree. Grace enables us to do difficult things in life because God is willing to give us what we don't deserve. God will give you the grace to move on from a toxic relationship.

Let God Fight for You

God loved Adam and the Woman; therefore, He confronted the Serpent. God loves you as well, and He will fight for you because He wants the best possible relationship with you and any relationship that is toxic for you is going to interfere with your relationship with God. Notice the stern words God says to the Serpent in Genesis 3:14, *"And the LORD God said unto the serpent,*

Because thou hast done this, thou art cursed above all cattle, and above every beast of the field; upon thy belly shalt thou go, and dust shalt thou eat all the days of thy life."

It would be miserable to crawl around on your belly for eternity. The point is that we must turn the toxic relationship and the toxic person over to God and let Him deal with them, while you focus your heart on your relationship with the Lord Jesus Christ.

Most Toxic People Will Always Be Toxic

Jesus said in John 10:10, *"The thief cometh not, but for to steal, and to kill, and to destroy . . . "* He spoke these words some four thousand years after the Serpent beguiled the Woman in the Garden of Eden. Since the beginning of time, Satan has not changed his ways, and most toxic people don't change their heart either. People can change their heart and improve their own lives through the grace of God, but unless God changes their lives, it is likely that they will always be toxic to you on some level.

No matter how your life has been affected by toxic relationships, you can live victoriously. Take inventory of Who loves you and eliminate the toxic people in your life. If you cannot completely eliminate them, you can at least take some control over their power of influence on your thoughts and emotions.

CHAPTER 21

Mastering our Emotions

"When a man is prey to his emotions, he is not his own master."

Benedict de Spinoza

Have you noticed that those who have no control over their anger, bitterness, vengeance, and hatred like to control the emotions of others? Genesis 3:1 begins with these solemn words, *"Now the serpent was more subtil than any beast of the field which the LORD God had made. And he said unto the woman, Yea, hath God said, Ye shall not eat of every tree of the garden?"*

The serpent was the creature Satan chose to possess for his evil work of deceiving the first humans. The word "subtle" means sly, artful, cunning, crafty, and deceitful. The serpent used craftiness in a deceitful way. By manipulating the Woman's emotions, he influenced her with his well-crafted words and reasoning and convinced her that God could not be trusted.

As Satan used emotions to manipulate the first woman for his own purpose, when we manipulate someone's emotions, it is because we are being selfish or because we have a purpose that is in some way destructive. Many people manipulate the emotions of others out of their own hurts and disappointments in life. Ultimately, Satan manipulated the Woman's emotions because he hated God and wanted to turn the first humans against the God that had created them. Satan's purpose and methods have not changed, and he continues with the same approach today.

So how can this information about emotions help us in our relationships? Let's begin by defining what we mean by emotions. "Emotion" is defined as a moving of the mind or soul; any agitation of mind or excitement of sensibility. Our emotions are our God-given instructive state of mind, and they can be affected by our circumstances, experiences, or relationships with others.

Our Emotional Purpose in Relationships

Our purpose in relationships should always be to nurture and edify one another. We find these truths clearly in what is referred to as the "one another's" of Scripture.

- Romans 15:14 - *"And I myself also am persuaded of you, my brethren, that ye also are full of goodness, filled with all knowledge, able also to admonish one another."*
- 1 John 4:11 - *"Beloved, if God so loved us, we ought also to love one another."*
- Galatians 6:2 - *"Bear ye one another's burdens, and so fulfil the law of Christ."*
- Ephesians 4:2 - *"With all lowliness and meekness, with longsuffering, forbearing one another in love."*
- Ephesians 4:32 - *"And be ye kind one to another, tenderhearted, forgiving one another, even as God for Christ's sake hath forgiven you."*
- Colossians 3:13 - *"Forbearing one another, and forgiving one another, if any man have a quarrel against any: even as Christ forgave you, so also do ye."*
- Colossians 3:16 - *"Let the word of Christ dwell in you richly in all wisdom; teaching and admonishing one another in psalms and hymns and spiritual songs, singing with grace in your hearts to the LORD."*
- 1 Thessalonians 4:18 - *"Wherefore comfort one another with these words."*
- 1 Thessalonians 5:11 - *"Wherefore comfort yourselves together, and edify one another, even as also ye do."*

- Hebrews 3:13 - *"But exhort one another daily, while it is called To day; lest any of you be hardened through the deceitfulness of sin."*

In these statements, we can see that God instructs us to love, admonish (counsel against wrong), bear one another's burdens, be forbearing (patient), kind, tenderhearted, forgiving, comforting, and edifying (building others up in Christian knowledge). These behaviors are what support emotionally healthy relationships.

The Emotions We Have Toward One Another

We sometimes have conflicts in our relationships, which result in our reacting emotionally, sometimes to a point of an emotional explosion. Throughout Scripture, we are admonished to not allow this to happen. The following is a list of destructive emotions that we must guard against:

- John 6:43 - *"Jesus therefore answered and said unto them, Murmur not among yourselves."*
- Galatians 5:15 - *"But if ye bite and devour one another, take heed that ye be not consumed one of another."*
- Galatians 5:26 - *"Let us not be desirous of vain glory, provoking one another, envying one another."*
- James 4:11 - *"Speak not evil one of another, brethren. He that speaketh evil of his brother, and judgeth his brother, speaketh evil of the law, and judgeth the law: but if thou judge the law, thou art not a doer of the law, but a judge."*
- James 5:9 - *"Grudge not one against another, brethren, lest ye be condemned: behold, the judge standeth before the door."*

Each of the behaviors in these verses comes from the negative emotions of anger, bitterness, jealousy, malice, hatred, and vengeance. These emotions are destructive to our relationships, and we must be careful to maintain control of them. If we do not control our emotions, Proverbs 15:18 says, *A wrathful man stirreth up strife: but he that is slow to anger appeaseth strife.*

Our emotions, whether negative or positive, will produce behaviors in our relationships. If we have the emotion of anger in our heart, we will bear negative fruit in our relationships because our heart will produce angry words and angry behaviors toward those we should love. If you are harboring anger, bitterness, or strife in your heart, you can expect to have challenges in your relationships.

Our Thoughts Affect Our Emotions

In Jeremiah 29:11, God said, *"For I know the thoughts that I think toward you, saith the LORD, thoughts of peace, and not of evil, to give you an expected end."* God's thoughts toward us are positive, hopeful, and filled with an expectation of good results for our lives. Although our minds are not pure like God's, we are told in Scripture to have the mind of Christ. Read Paul's words carefully from Philippians 2:1-5, *"If there be therefore any consolation in Christ, if any comfort of love, if any fellowship of the Spirit, if any bowels* (affections) *and mercies, fulfil ye my joy, that ye be likeminded, having the same love, being of one accord, of one mind. Let nothing be done through strife or vainglory; but in lowliness of mind let each esteem other better than themselves. Look not every man on his own things, but every man also on the things of others. Let this mind be in you, which was also in Christ Jesus."*

If we decide to have thoughts of love, forgiveness, hope, mercy, and compassion in our heart, then we will bear positive fruit in our words and actions.

Truth Balances Our Emotions

We all know that emotions can be confusing and can't always be trusted. It has been my experience that people who have experienced trauma often struggle to understand, trust, and control their emotions. The great equalizer of our emotions is truth, because truth never changes. When we are struggling with emotions in our relationships, it is wise to take the time to examine our emotions in light of truth. Are there negative emotions in your heart that you need to confront and put away to improve the situation?

Whether you are dealing with old issues in your heart from past relationships or just struggling in some way with your emotions, search the Scriptures and seek wise counsel. There are answers, and you can have happier relationships by dealing with your negative emotions.

CHAPTER 22

Communication in Our Relationships

"The most important thing in communication is to hear what isn't being said."

Peter Drucker, *The Effective Executive*

Communication is defined as imparting thoughts or opinions, and conversation is defined as the general course of manners, behavior, and intimate fellowship or association. By this definition, we know that communication is both verbal and non-verbal. We communicate verbally through conversations in person or through our communication devices, and we communicate nonverbally through our facial expressions, body language, behavior, manners, actions, and reactions.

One of the biggest challenges in our relationships is communication which primarily involves conversation, too often the wrong conversation. Wrong conversations are ones that have the wrong purpose. They come from hearts that are angry, bitter, and contemptuous instead of healing, forgiving, reconciliatory, and compassionate.

Dangers of Not Communicating

In a relationship, when communication starts to fade, everything else follows. Just as good communication will reap its blessings, no communication will also reap its own fruits. It is through communication and interaction that we bond with others and develop trust. Without communication, the relationship will be weak.

Communication also reveals what is in each other's hearts. Without communication we will make assumptions, and we will won't understand or be understood, adding stress to the relationship. Not communicating also produces bad feelings such as anger, bitterness, and resentment in those close to us because basic emotional needs are not being.

Without communication, we will turn inward and adopt an attitude of solitude. I know more than one person who is married but lonely. Often, when this occurs, one or both members of the relationship will search for a surrogate. A surrogate is someone we put in the place of another. When a spouse feels that their needs are not being met, they may search out a surrogate to have those needs fulfilled. A child, friend, or employee may search for a surrogate as well if his or her emotional needs are not being fulfilled.

Learning to Communicate

Most of our communication skills are learned from the environment we grow up in. I have seen married couples who only tolerate each other, disconnected because somewhere along the way they stopped communicating or never really communicated well to begin with. Unfortunately, their children probably won't learn to communicate either, and the lack of communication or the lack of knowing how to communicate can be brought into every relationship the children have later on in life. Fortunately, it is never too late to improve ourselves and our communication skills.

Begin with a Conversation with Yourself

The first recorded conversation in Scripture took place between the Trinity in Genesis 1:26 when God the Father said to God the Son and God the Holy Spirit, *"Let us make man in our image after our likeness . . . "* This example illustrates an important principle for us: When we desire to improve a relationship through communication, the first conversation we need to have should be with ourselves. We need to examine our own attitudes, actions, communication practices, and responses. Most importantly, we should look into our own heart and confront any unresolved issues that are making it difficult for us to have a good relationship with ourselves and others.

The best way to improve any relationship is to begin with improving yourself, so take a close look at your own image, what do you see? What do you need to change to make your relationships better? Are you living in the likeness of Jesus Christ?

To begin that conversation of examining yourself, I suggest praying King David's prayer from Psalm 139:23–24, *"Search me, O God, and know my heart: try me, and know my thoughts: And see if there be any wicked way in me, and lead me in the way everlasting."*

The Right Purpose of Communication

The purpose of God's communication with us is to grow our relationship with Him, to help us in our daily living, and to provide stability, security, confidence, and companionship. Our communication and conversations need to have a purpose as well. We need to listen to each other, and we need to express ourselves to each other in order to fulfill our basic human needs. Sometimes we don't even realize that our needs are being met through communication, but how many times have you walked away from a conversation with someone and thought to yourself, "That was a great conversation. It felt good to talk with that person." The reason for feeling this way is simple: A need to communicate with other human beings was fulfilled in the conversation and the conversation fulfilled its right purpose.

The Right Heart Attitude in Communication

Colossians 4:6 says, *"Let your speech be always with grace, seasoned with salt, that ye may know how ye ought to answer every man."* To achieve speaking with grace, we must have a right heart attitude toward others in our communication. If we are harboring anger, bitterness, or contempt for the people with whom we communicate, we are going to have trouble. Whether our objective is to resolve conflict, understand, be understood, or become better acquainted, we must strive to have a right heart attitude toward the person we are communicating to.

Understand and Be Understood

We are not mind readers, so we must communicate in order to understand and be understood. When we are dealing with challenges in our relationships, we usually focus on the weaknesses or shortcomings of the other party, and we think we need to "fix" them. What we really need, however, is to sit down and have a conversation and seek to understand each other and to be understood.

Right conversation and right communication is important because it is the way we understand each other, but there is more to it than just having a conversation. We must hear each other, and we must give the other party the opportunity and liberty to express their true thoughts and emotions. To accomplish this requires that we try to put ourselves in their place, to walk in their shoes, and to attempt to see life from their perspective. When we are seeking to understand one another in our relationships, then we know we can go to one another and obtain mercy, grace, and help in time of need. Through understanding, our relationships grow!

Guard the Content of Conversations

Take a look at the first recorded conversation God had with the first man in Genesis 1:27–28, *"So God created man in His own image, in the image of God created He him; male and female created He them. And God blessed them, and God said unto them, Be fruitful, and multiply, and replenish the earth, and subdue it: and have dominion over the fish of the sea, and over the fowl of the air, and over every living thing that moveth upon the earth."*

The blessing God placed on Adam and the Woman was an expression of love and adoration, a pronouncement of happiness and success. The content of the first conversation was positive. The content of our conversations should always be positive and edifying in nature. While the actual content will also be determined by the nature of the conversation, it is helpful if we try to guide our conversations in the right direction. By understanding the purpose of the conversation, we can better guard the content of the conversation and ensure the conversation is productive.

CHAPTER 23

Setting Goals

"If you don't know where you are going, you might wind up someplace else."

Yogi Berra

Our mission statement for this book is "We believe you CAN have good relationships." We realize that no relationship is ever going to be perfect because none of us are perfect, but our relationships can be good. If both parties are willing to work together on the common goal to make things better, the relationship can improve.

For several years, I have practiced and taught on personal goals for life. The basics of the lesson are to categorize your goals and have a goal for six areas of life:

- Spiritual
- Health
- Personal Growth
- Vocational
- Financial
- Relationship

In this chapter, I want to share some principles on setting goals for growth in relationships.

Prioritize Prayer

Whenever we pray about anything, we are involving God in our lives. Praying about our relationships is the most important thing we can do to strengthen and improve them. Ask God to show you how you can improve the relationship, ask for wisdom, and ask God to show you what your goal should be for the relationship. If you are uncertain how to pray, consider answering some questions for yourself and then lift the answers to these questions to God in prayer.

- What is the biggest challenge in the relationship?
- Do we need reconciliation?
- Is there something I need to improve in my own life? If so, what is it?
- What am I missing?
- What needs do the other party have?

Don't overlook the importance and power of prayer. Once you have prayed and set a goal for the relationship, continue to pray about the relationship as you work toward your goal.

Secure the Goal in Your Heart

We can make all kinds of lists, and we can write down hundreds of goals; however, the most important place to write any goal down is on your own heart. The goal must become a desire of your heart. King David said, *"Delight thyself also in the LORD: and He shall give thee the desires of thine heart"* (Psalm 37:4). When it comes to improving our closest relationships, we need more than just an, "I hope things get better" approach. Rather, we need to have a genuine desire, faith, and willingness to act to improve our relationships. Whatever your desires are for your marriage, your children, or others, securely fix those desires in your heart and pursue them.

Claim a Bible Verse for Your Goal

My mentor and former pastor Dr. Charles Keen taught me to select a Bible verse for any ministry or endeavor I desire to pursue, and I believe Dr.

Keen would agree that improving our relationships is an important endeavor. Chose a Bible verse or passage that speaks to your heart and use that verse as the goal for your relationship. Here are some great verses to get you started:

- 1 Corinthians 13:4–7 - *"Charity suffereth long, an] is kind; charity envieth not; charity vaunteth not itself, is not puffed up, doth not behave itself unseemly, seeketh not her own, is not easily provoked, thinketh no evil; rejoiceth not in iniquity, but rejoiceth in the truth; beareth all things, believeth all things, hopeth all things, endureth all things."*
- 1 Thessalonians 5:11 - *"Wherefore comfort yourselves together, and edify one another, even as also ye do."*
- Ephesians 4:2 - *"With all lowliness and meekness, with longsuffering, forbearing one another in love."*
- Matthew 7:2 - *"For with what judgment ye judge, ye shall be judged: and with what measure ye mete, it shall be measured to you again."*
- Philippians 2:3 - *"Let nothing be done through strife or vainglory; but in lowliness of mind let each esteem other better than themselves."*

Follow Jesus' teaching and search the Scriptures, find the passage that speaks to you, and claim it for yourself toward improving your relationships.

Write the Goal on Paper

There are many good reasons why you want to write all your goals down on paper. Writing your goal on paper helps you think it through. Writing it down also gives you a point of reference and helps you stay focused as you review it every day. I encourage you write your goals down on paper and read it several times a day. Doing so can uplift you when you are discouraged or struggling with the way things are going.

Commit to the Goal

Praying about the relationship, making the goal a desire of your heart, claiming a Bible passage, and writing it down on paper are all steps toward committing to the relationship goal. Now, commit yourself to the goal and to the person for which you have made the goal. This is a commitment you must make in your own heart to yourself and to God. Committing yourself to the goal will help you stay motivated to work toward the goal. If it is appropriate, share the goal with the other party. Let them know they are important to you and that you are committed to them and to improving your relationship with them.

Enlist Help

Enlisting help may include seeking counsel about the relationship either on your own or with the other party. As always, I suggest that you only seek counsel from your pastor or a Christian counselor as they will help you set proper relationship goals from the Scriptures and find healing. Seeking out a mentor who can encourage you can help you improve yourself and achieve your relationship goals.

Work Toward the Goal Every Day

I was once in a Bible class, and the teacher asked the question, "Which swing of an axe cuts down a tree?"

I thought for a moment and answered in my mind, the last one. But that was wrong. The correct answer was, "All of them." It takes every swing of an ax to cut down a tree, no matter the size of the tree.

If you had a large tree you needed to cut down and you went to the tree every day and took five swings at the tree, eventually, the tree would fall. We can improve ourselves and our relationships, but we must keep our axe sharp, and we must be consistent in chopping at the root of our challenges. Be consistent and work toward your relationship goals!

CHAPTER 24

The Best Relationship

There is one relationship that excels all other relationships, and that is our relationship with God through His only begotten Son Jesus Christ. As we shared at the beginning of this book, God created us for the purpose of a relationship, and He created you personally for the purpose of a relationship with Him.

John 3:16, one of the most famous verses in the Bible, says *"For God so loved the world, that He gave His only begotten Son, that whosoever believeth in Him should not perish, but have everlasting life."*

First John 4:10 says, *"Herein is love, not that we loved God, but that He loved us, and sent His Son to be the propitiation for our sins."*

The first humans, Adam and Eve, disobeyed God and sinned against Him, bringing the curse of sin upon the entire human race. Despite our sin, God still loves us, and He desires a relationship with us. He expressed His love for you in sending Jesus Christ to be the sin sacrifice on the cross. While suffering on the cross, Jesus Christ shed His blood and gave His life so every sin you have ever committed or ever will commit could be forgiven and so you could have a personal relationship with Him.

Matthew 11:28–30 says, *"Come unto me, all ye that labour and are heavy laden, and I will give you rest. Take my yoke upon you, and learn of me; for I am meek and lowly in heart: and ye shall find rest unto your souls. For my yoke is easy, and my burden is light."* What a wonderful invitation from Jesus! He invites you to enter a relationship with Him in which He will give you rest, share your burdens, and encourage your heart.

In your relationship with God, you have Someone you can go to with life decisions, Someone Who loves you unconditionally, Someone Who wants to share your burdens, and Someone Who will never leave you or forsake you. In Him, you have a friend with Whom you can converse with daily, yet He is not just anyone—He is the Creator of the universe and the One Who created you for the very purpose of having a relationship, the best relationship you could ever have. Will you respond to God's invitation to have a relationship with Him?

Here is how you can respond to the invitation:

Believe with the sincerity of your heart.

In John 5:24 Jesus said, *"Verily, verily, I say unto you, he that heareth my word, and believeth on Him that sent Me, hath everlasting life, and shall not come into condemnation; but is passed from death unto life.* Romans 10:9–10 says, *"That if thou shalt confess with thy mouth the LORD Jesus, and shalt believe in thine heart that God hath raised Him from the dead, thou shalt be saved. For with the heart man believeth unto righteousness; and with the mouth confession is made unto salvation."* This is an important matter in all of our close relationships, and it is especially important in our relationship with God. The heart is our most inner being; it is the center of who we are.

The things we sincerely believe in our heart are the things we live by, they are the things that guide our decisions, and they are the things we grow by. Entering a relationship with God is something that must come from your heart. It is more than praying a prayer; it is more than making a change in your life. A heart relationship with God is a transformation of your life through believing on Jesus Christ as your personal Saviour!

Like other relationships, our relationship with God begins with a level of trust, by believing that Jesus Christ is the Son of God, believing that He loves you, and believing that He shed His blood on the cross, died for your sins, and rose again three days later.

God does not expect us to understand all of this, but He does ask us to trust Him, to believe in Him and His Son Jesus Christ.

Repent

Repent means that we realize we have trespassed against God and that we are sorry for our trespasses. It also means that we now want to turn from our sin and ourselves and toward God. To repent is to change our mind and direction from ourselves toward a relationship with God through Jesus Christ.

Confess

To confess means to acknowledge that you have done something wrong. Romans 10:9 says, *"That if thou shalt confess with thy mouth the LORD Jesus, and shalt believe in thine heart that God hath raised Him from the dead, thou shalt be saved."* We enter a relationship with God by acknowledging that we have trespassed against Him and that we need His forgiveness, His salvation, and a relationship with Him. God invites you to enter a relationship with Him through faith and I encourage you to turn to Him now, confess your sin to Him, and believe on Jesus Christ with your heart.

A Sample Prayer of Salvation

There are no specific words that you must recite or chant in order to enter a personal relationship with Jesus Christ. The most important thing is that you sincerely believe in your heart on Jesus Christ. Below, however, is a model prayer, if you need help with the words to say to accept Jesus' invitation of salvation:

> Dear God, I confess that I have sinned and trespassed against You. I now turn from myself and my sin and turn to You with my heart. I believe that You love me and that Jesus Christ is Your

only begotten Son and that He shed His blood and died on the Cross for my sins. I further believe that He resurrected on the third day. I place my faith in Jesus Christ's finished work of the cross for my personal salvation and for a personal relationship with You. Amen!

If you have believed on Jesus as your Saviour, then you have a personal relationship with Him! This is the best relationship you will ever have; thus, be sure to cultivate the relationship and grow closer to Him through praying to Him, reading the Bible, and worshipping Him. God bless you!

Bibliography

An Exposition of the Old Testament by John Gill, Publisher: W. Clowes for Mathews & Leigh, 1810 London.

The Weight Of Glory And Other Addresses C. S. Lewis, Publisher: Wm. B. Eerdmans Publishing Co, 1965-01-01.

For more information about

Dr. Don Woodard
and
Life's About Relationships
please visit:

www.drdonwoodard.com

Ambassador International's mission is to magnify the Lord Jesus Christ
and promote His gospel through the written word.

We believe through the publication of Christian literature, Jesus Christ and
His Word will be exalted, believers will be strengthened in their walk with
Him, and the lost will be directed to Jesus Christ as the only way of salvation

For more information about
AMBASSADOR INTERNATIONAL
please visit:

www.ambassador-international.com

*Thank you for reading this book. Please consider leaving us a
review on your social media, favorite retailer's website,
Goodreads or Bookbub, or our website.*

More from Ambassador International . . .

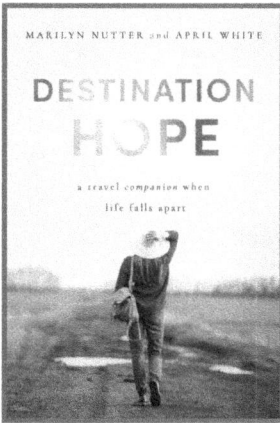

Destination Hope is a must-read invaluable guide, offering hope and sound wisdom for your unpredictable, individual life journeys. Written by two of the wisest tried, tested, and true women of God—April White and Marilyn Nutter—you will see how each author poured out beautiful transparency. Like two best friends who've trailed the hard ground before you, April and Marilyn, seem to gently take you by the hand and lead you toward God's heart for healing.

In *Transformed Thinking*, Tom Wheeler clearly lays out the most fundamental beliefs of Christianity and compares them to other worldviews, providing arguments to support his beliefs. Even though this book is purposed for the classroom setting, it would be a beneficial read for any believer who wants to have a firm foundation on which to share their beliefs with unbelievers.

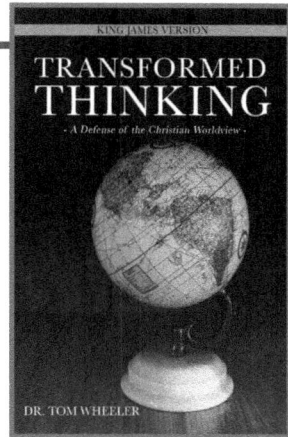

Combining his experiences as a secular business manager, church staff member, and Christian leader, Matt applies practical principles from God's Word in *How to Be a Team Player and Enjoy It* on topics such as management positions and subordinate positions, communication amongst the different tiers of leadership, time management, and on desiring to love and serve others as Jesus did.

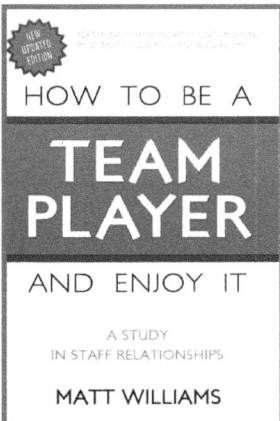